How to Play
Good Opening Moves

How to Play
Good Opening Moves

Edmar Mednis
International Grandmaster

David McKay Company, Inc.
New York

Library of Congress Cataloging in Publication Data

Mednis, Edmar, 1937–
    How to play good opening moves.

    1. Chess—Openings   I. Title.
GV1450.M42   794.1′22   82–197
ISBN 0–679–14109-X   AACR2

5 6 7 8 9 10

MANUFACTURED IN THE UNITED STATES OF AMERICA

To my sisters, Aiga and Inita

Preface

There is no shortage of books published on the chess openings. The reasons are clear: the opening is a very important part of the game, and a tremendous amount of technical material is readily available. By their very nature these books are encyclopedic and are concerned with a single opening or various groups of openings. Since opening theory is expanding very rapidly, such books invariably contain material that has become obsolete even before the books themselves have been published. Nevertheless, they are indispensable for the professional master, both for reference purposes and as a starting point for his or her independent studies. The best series of such books is the five-volume *Encyclopedia of Chess Openings.*

But what of the chess player who enjoys chess and wants to improve his or her competitive success, but has neither the time nor inclination to memorize hundreds of variations? What he or she really needs is guidance on how to obtain good positions in the opening *without* relying on reams of memorized analysis. This book is aimed at exactly this type of player and uses the techniques that I have developed in many years of successful group and private teaching. The emphasis throughout is on principles. Starting with the very first move, the reader learns how to select good opening moves just by observing the three primary principles of good opening play.

Since the book's approach is an original one, most of the research material is original also. The rest has been obtained from what can be considered the standard sources: personal contacts, leading chess periodicals, books. When appropriate, credit is given in the text. As with all of my previous books, my partner here too has been my wonderful blonde wife Baiba. My deepest gratitude goes to her for typing the entire manuscript and for continuous moral support.

The following list contains the standard meanings of the symbols used throughout the text:

```
!  = a strong move
!! = a very strong move; a fantastic move
?  = a bad move; a weak move
?? = a horrible move; a blunder
!? = an enterprising move; a move worthy of consideration
?! = a dubious move, for theoretical or practical reasons
```

Since this book is about principles rather than analysis, technical chess errors should be at a minimum. Still, given the complexity and inexhaustability of chess, some errors are almost inevitable. The author accepts responsibility for all of these. Your assistance in bringing them to my attention will be appreciated.

New York, 1982   Edmar Mednis

Contents

How to Play
Good Opening Moves

CHAPTER 1
What Is the Opening?

SECTION 1. General Considerations

The beginning phase of a game of chess is called the opening. What is the relative importance of the opening as compared to the middlegame and endgame? The question can be argued from various points of view, yet there is no definitive answer—the complete chess player should aim to be equally adept at all these phases. Nevertheless, a valid case can be made that the study of openings should be the first area undertaken. The Germans have an expression which translated goes something like: "A good opening means that the game is half won." Such a saying should not be taken too literally, yet its point is well taken. Gaining an advantage early is not only of obvious practical value but is also significant psychologically. If you know that you stand well, this should give you confidence during the action to come; conversely, your opponent, realizing that he stands badly, may not be able to pull himself together to face the ensuing middlegame. Thus, an opening advantage can well lead to an easy win in the middlegame.

What have some of the leading players in chess history expected to get out of the opening? J.R. Capablanca considered the main principle to be "rapid and efficient development," with the corollary being that when the pieces are brought out, they must be "put in the right places." He also gives some excellent advice about what to do when confronted with an unfamiliar move—as happens many times to everyone!—: "Play what you might call the common-sense move." By this he means following the general principle stated above; even if the move played may not turn out to be the very best one (usually subsequent analysis is

1

required to discover this), the plan of aiming to bring out the pieces quickly to safe locations will in the large majority of cases produce a perfectly *good* move.

Larry Evans provides a modern technical definition when he says "The opening is a fight for space, time and force." Svetozar Gligoric emphasizes the factor of time, being concerned with the rate at which the chess pieces enter the fight. According to him, "The efficient use of time in the opening requires generally that each move should be used to develop a new piece." Lajos Portisch presents a more philosophical outlook, painting with a broad brush, as it were: "Your only task in the opening is to reach a playable middlegame." Anatoly Karpov's games show that he is in basic agreement with Portisch's thesis. Robert J. Fischer's approach to the opening is a very demanding one: if possible, he prefers to sweep his opponent off the board at the very start.

Of course, the specific goals for White and Black are different. Success in the opening for White means that he emerges with at least a slight pull. Black, on the other hand, can feel completely satisfied if he has equalized. Both Fischer and Karpov have been very successful in retaining at least some of White's natural advantage. Playing Black against them has always been a most disagreeable task. Karpov's goal with Black has changed considerably since he became world champion in 1975. Formerly, when playing against world class grandmasters, he was satisfied in eventually obtaining safe, sound equality and a draw. But as World Champion he is interested in winning every game, and, therefore, his openings with Black have become considerably more dynamic.

For Fischer, dynamic positions have invariably been the rule. That's why his main weapons for Black have always been the Najdorf Sicilian against 1 P–K4 and the King's Indian and Grüenfeld against 1 P–Q4. These opening systems require exceedingly accurate play from White, lest the initiative pass to Black. Fischer enjoys such situations and is always ready to seize whatever chance is offered. Nevertheless, his primary concern is to play sound chess, doing whatever the position requires. If White's play is perfect, he realizes that it will take some time before he can equalize. There is seldom any unjustified outburst of activity in his games. As Robert Byrne tells it, they had a session of analysis together in the late 1960's in which Fischer, in looking over some of Byrne's games, expressed surprise whenever he noticed that Byrne was jumping the gun in playing for the attack with the Black pieces. Disapprovingly, Fischer advised: "You've got to equalize first with Black before looking for something."

In general, it is safe to say that White should aim for at least some advantage out of the opening, whereas Black should strive for equality. Depending on whether Black's primary goal is to win or to draw, his aim should be either dynamic or safe equality. Does this mean that no other move except that which official theory currently considers the best may be played? Of course not—other moves or plans are often valid for either psychological or practical reasons. For instance, the anticipated effect of some surprising move on an opponent who is known to feel uncomfortable when taken out of theory may be of great practical value. Or a player may know, understand, and enjoy playing a line which theoreticians regard as slightly inferior. No matter—each player is well advised to play whatever opening he likes and understands best. What is important, though, is to keep a certain logical perspective on one's approach. It is simply foolhardy for White *voluntarily* to choose a line which—if Black plays correctly—hands the initiative over to the opponent. Experimentation by White should be limited to those moves where the ultimate result is no worse than equality. Black for his part shouldn't risk a line where—if White plays correctly—Black will wind up so far behind the eight ball that his chances for recovery are slight. Experimentation by Black should be limited to moves where White's resulting advantage is slight, with at most an additional marginal inferiority for Black as compared to the theoretically best lines.

How long is the opening? The dividing line between the end of the opening and the start of the middlegame is not a sharp one. Many of the current books on openings present analysis often running into move 20 and beyond. It should be clear that in such cases the game has already entered the middle stage. A simple yardstick is that when the initial piece development has been accomplished, we are ready for the middlegame. Normally this occurs within the first 10–15 moves. Alternatively, we can consider the opening over when at least one of the players has accomplished a majority of the specific objectives of opening play. These objectives or goals are discussed in the next section.

The ultimate key to successful play is understanding chess. Though a fair amount of specific knowledge is required in the opening, still it is of considerably greater value to understand how to play good opening moves, rather than to have memorized lots of complicated variations. Capablanca, as he himself readily admitted, was not an expert in formal opening theory. In 1919 at Havana a match was arranged between him and the Serbian master Kostic, who was noted for his great opening memorization. As Capa described him then: "Kostic knows by heart every game played by a master in the last twenty years, and a considerable number of games of much older date." Nevertheless, Capablanca was not in the least daunted, and, with his much deeper chess understanding, swept the first five games. His great opening knowledge notwithstanding, Kostic thereupon resigned the match.

SECTION 2. Specific Principles

As a science progresses from its infancy to widespread acceptance, tenets that seemed at first to be grounded in witchcraft are replaced by those based on logic and verified by experimentation. This is the stage that chess has reached today. The basic principles are agreed to and understood by the leading scientists (top players). It can be stated with a high degree of confidence that the basic principles of opening play will not be superseded by new discoveries in the foreseeable future. These principles have obtained a kind of universality. Thus, the principles described in this book will remain valid for at least the next one hundred years.

This does not mean, however, that the age of discovery is over. If anything, just the opposite is true. Many new opening schemes are still to be discovered, and our understanding of many present openings increased. As more is learned about certain presently unpopular or unsatisfactory systems, some of these may well be rehabilitated. The direction of discovery should, however, be generally positive. I expect that many new good plans will be established. There is no reason, however, to think that any present lines that are based on both sound logic and practical successes will suddenly be proven unsound. Therefore, the tools presented in this book for learning how to find good opening moves will remain valid. The good moves will remain good; the progress of opening theory will lead to the discovery of more good moves.

The three areas of greatest significance for opening play are King safety, piece development and center control. The importance of the King is not a controversial matter, and the need for its safety in the middlegame is well recognized. It is important, moreover, to keep the King's safety in mind from the very first move. It is false security to think that just because the opponent doesn't have many pieces out, one's King must be safe. The counterpoint here is that the potential defenders of the King are also not yet mobilized. A sudden end can befall even the White King. Two grotesque examples: (1) 1 P–KB4 P–K3 2 P–KN4?? Q–R5mate; (2) 1 P–Q4 N–KB3 2 N–Q2?! P–K4!? 3 PxP N–N5 4 P–KR3?? N–K6!! and White resigned in a game between two French masters, since the "necessary" 5 PxN allows 5 . . . Q–R5ch 6 P–KN3 QxNPmate.

The logic of rapid and purposeful development has been referred to earlier and at this point needs no further discussion.

The value and importance of the center is not, however, sufficiently appreciated by a majority of chess amateurs. The center and the control thereof is of utmost significance both in the opening and the middlegame. If we consider such popular sports as basketball, ice hockey, football or soccer, we see that most of the action is concentrated in the center of the field. Local skirmishes may take place in the corners, ends or sides, but the grand plays generally begin at or near the center. A similar situation exists in chess. The exact center in chess consists of the squares Q4, K4, Q5, K5 (shown enclosed within solid lines on Diagram 1), and these are the four squares of maximum importance. They are called the *primary* central squares. Also of considerable importance are the squares adjoining these primary squares. These are called the *secondary* central squares and form the larger square QB3–QB6–KB6–KB3, as shown by the dotted lines in Diagram 1.

Viewed strictly from the standpoint of central importance, the secondary central squares along the QB file are equivalent to those along the KB file. Therefore, it would seem to be just as logical to use the respective KBPs for central action and support as it is to

DIAGRAM 1

BLACK

WHITE

*Primary and secondary
central squares*

utilize the QBPs for this purpose. Yet when we recall the need for King safety we see that this is not so, since moving the KBP of necessity loosens the King position. This is always a factor with the King still uncastled and may be of some significance even when the King has castled Kingside. This of course does *not* mean that the use of the KBP for central purposes is taboo, yet whenever such use is contemplated one must feel sure that the advantage to be gained in the center is not outweighed by the decreased safety of the King. No such constraints exist for the utilization of the QBP, unless it is anticipated that Queenside castling will or must be performed. It also follows from the above discussion that weaknesses of squares on the KB file in the vicinity of one's own King are of potentially greater danger than similar weaknesses on the Queenside, i.e., vulnerability at KB2, KB3 and KB4 is more serious than at QB2, QB3, QB4. In general: the QBP is a natural instrument for central action, but before employing the KBP for this purpose, make sure that the King remains safe.

The importance of controlling the center has been known to those following chess theory ever since Wilhelm Steinitz started to expound on strategic principles in the late 19th century. At that time control of center was synonymous with actual possession.

DIAGRAM 2

BLACK

WHITE

*Control of
White's Q4 square*

Thus, for example, to control White's Q4, it was thought White must either have a protected pawn or piece there. It was the Hypermodern school of the 1920's that significantly deepened our understanding of central play. What mattered, according to them, was not possession but control, and it may be even advantageous to achieve this from long range! In synthesizing the ultimate truths of the classic teachers and the hypermoderns, we have indeed learned that the center and its control are of major importance. What our free thinking has taught us is that how we accomplish this is usually irrelevant. If we again consider the white Q4 square in Diagram 2, any and all of the following methods for controlling it are of equivalent value:

(1) 1 P–Q4
(2) 1 P–K3
(3) 1 N–KB3
(4) 1 P–QN3, followed by 2 B–QN2
(5) 1 P–QB3

For realizing the advantage of the first move, White can do better than alternatives (2) and (5). However, for the purpose of controlling Q4 all are valid. As a particular opening is played and the need develops to control Q4, any one of them can be considered with a clear chess conscience.

With the above background in mind it is now possible to formulate the following three principles of correct opening play:

(1) Bring your King to safety by castling.
(2) Develop your pieces toward the center so that they are ready for middlegame action.
(3) Control the center, by either (1) actual possession or (2) short-range or long-range action of pieces or pawns.

The specific quality of various opening moves will be considered in the next two chapters. One overriding standard must be emphasized: unless an opening move works towards at least one of the above objectives, it will not be a good move.

CHAPTER 2
Quality of White Opening Moves

Section 1. Perfect Moves

Why not the best? According to current chess understanding, five of White's possible first moves are absolutely perfect, and there is no valid reason for not choosing one of them to start the game with. Though these moves are of equivalent quality, the nature of possible play arising from them can be quite varied, so that all kinds of individual styles can be accommodated by these "perfect five." From ultra sharp to safe and stodgy—choose your move and system, and attain the most promising position possible within your chosen field!

These perfect moves are shown by the arrows in Diagram 3. In the order of most to least active they are:

1 P–K4

The most active move. White puts a pawn on the important K4 square, thereby also exerting pressure on Q5. Diagonals are opened for the Queen and KB and a rapid deployment of the latter becomes possible. Development of the KN and KB allows for rapid Kingside castling. Generally open and active play is the characteristic of openings resulting from 1 P–K4. This move is useful towards achieving all three opening objectives.

1 P–Q4

This can be considered as the Queenside counterpart to 1 P–K4.

DIAGRAM 3

BLACK

WHITE

*The five perfect
first moves for White*

White puts a pawn on the important Q4 square, thereby also exerting pressure on K5. A diagonal is opened for the QB and a bit of a file for the Queen. Immediate play arising from 1 P–Q4 is usually concerned with the center and Queenside. Two of the opening objectives are served by it. Active strategic play is the major characteristic of openings resulting from 1 P–Q4.

1 P–QB4 (English Opening)

On the face of it this may not seem to be of major usefulness since only the Queen's development is furthered. Its principal value comes from the pressure it exerts on Q5, to be reinforced by the logical follow-up of 2 N–QB3. Then the QN is able to exert maximum central pressure, while the QBP has also been already mobilized for this purpose. When taking into account the continuation 2 N–QB3, it can be seen that 1 P–QB4 serves to further two of the opening objectives. Play in the English Opening usually develops on the Queenside, with the Queen often making use of the QR4, QN3 and QB2 squares. The English is a fairly active strategic opening.

1 N–KB3

This move is ideal from the standpoint of opening principles, as it furthers all three objectives. Unless he later chooses to transpose into some other opening, White will continue with 2 P–KN3, 3 B–N2 and 4 0–0. In just four moves White will then have castled, exerted actual central pressure with the KN and latent pressure with the KB. Admittedly this is not an aggressive plan, yet it is fully in accordance with modern opening principles. Often games started with 1 N–KB3 transpose into other lines: following up with 2 P–Q4 leads to QP openings, while the continuation 2 P–QB4 can lead to the English.

1 P–KN3

This appears passive, yet it also helps to achieve all three opening objectives. After 2 B–N2 the Bishop controls the important K4 and Q5 central squares. As a follow-up, White can pay further attention to the Q5 square by playing 3 P–QB4 and 4 N–QB3, or he can complete Kingside development with 3 N–KB3 and 4 0–0. As can be seen, 1 P–KN3 is a very flexible move and—though not active—is nevertheless perfect.

There is a sixth first move which is almost perfect and is just a shade below the previous five in value. This is the Queenside counterpart of 1 P–KN3: 1 P–QN3. After 2 B–QN2 White will have sound pressure against the key Q4 and K5 squares. In the late 1960's and early 1970's Bent Larsen was very successful with 1 P–QN3, and it is deservedly named after him. However, extensive theoretical work has shown that 1 P–QN3 is somewhat inferior to 1 P–KN3 for the following two reasons:

(1) It does not further the safety of the King by preparing Kingside castling. (Queenside castling is not attractive in this opening.)
(2) Additional pressure on K5 is difficult to achieve, since P–KB4 would lead to some weakening of the King position.

Section 2. Mediocre Moves

If a person doesn't want to play the best, then at the very least he should choose one of the three mediocre possibilities. Each of them does have positive features, but because of inherent deficiencies, the highest rating that can be given them is "mediocre." These are shown in Diagram 4 and are:

DIAGRAM 4

BLACK

WHITE

*The three mediocre
first moves for White*

1 P–QN4

With the plan of 2 B–QN2, aiming at the Q4 and K5 squares. In addition, the pawn controls the secondary central QB5 square. It is unprotected, however, and after such normal responses as 1 . . . P–K3 or 1 . . . P–K4 White will soon have to take time out for P–QR3. Note that the same central purposes are served equally well by 1 P–QN3, and with *no* disadvantages.

1 N–QB3

The QN is placed on its best central square. By precluding the utilization of the QBP for central purposes, however, White makes it more difficult to establish a fully harmonious central/ piece–development combination. It is just too early to say on move one "I won't use the QBP."

1 P–KB4

This move contributes nothing to development and slightly weakens the Kingside. Its redeeming feature is that it serves to exert pressure on the central K5 square.

SECTION 3. Poor Moves

All other opening moves are poor. Don't play them! A brief comment about each of them is all that is necessary:

1 P–QR3, 1 P–QR4—These moves waste time.
1 N–QR3, 1 N–KR3—Both develop the Knight *away* from the center.
1 P–KR3, 1 P–KR4—These waste time *and* weaken the Kingside.
1 P–KB3—This does nothing for development and weakens the Kingside.
1 P–KN4—Seriously weakens the Kingside.
1 P–QB3, 1 P–K3, 1 P–Q3—Unnecessarily passive. These are reasonable moves for Black but make no sense for White. White should play as White, not as Black!

Since I don't want you to play them, I haven't shown them on any diagram!

CHAPTER 3
Quality of Black Opening Moves

In general we can say that what is good for White will also be good for Black, and what is poor for White will be even worse for Black. For instance, all of White's five perfect first moves are so good that Black can in each case respond symmetrically! On the other hand, the move 1 . . . P–KN4 is akin to suicide. Of course, White's first move can inhibit certain responses and reduce the value of others. The following sections will show how Black should and should not play. In all cases, I shall assume that White opened only with the perfect moves. If White has done otherwise, Black should play the same good moves—what will happen is that Black will get an excellent position in less time!

SECTION 1. Perfect Moves

Perfect moves will be those which help to further at least one of our stated opening objectives, while having no strategic or tactical deficiencies. Just as in Chapter 2, we shall discuss them in order, dealing first with the replies to White's most active moves.

A) 1 P–K4

Black has the following seven perfect responses, as shown in Diagram 5:

DIAGRAM 5

BLACK

WHITE

*Black's seven perfect
replies to 1 P–K4*

1 . . . P–QB3

Though incidentally freeing a diagonal for the Queen, the primary purpose of 1 . . . P–QB3 is to establish control of Black's Q4 square. Black plans 2 . . . P–Q4, so that after, e.g., 2 P–Q4 P–Q4 3 PxP PxP! his central control is equal to White's. Thus 1 . . . P–QB3 is not only centrally motivated but also prepares a challenge to White's active KP. It is a safe and sound opening, called the Caro-Kann Defense, and is popular with careful strategists. Former World Champion Tigran Petrosian has been a steady practitioner, and the present Champion, Anatoly Karpov, selected it for his 1974 match with Spassky.

1 . . . P–QB4

Black immediately exerts pressure on White's Q4 and is ready to intensify this with . . . N–QB3. This is the world–famous Sicilian Defense, once Robert J. Fischer's exclusive defense to 1 P–K4 and currently Black's most popular response to 1 P–K4. We shall take a close look at this important opening in Chapters 5 and 6.

1 . . . P–Q3

Black protects the K4 square and opens his QB's diagonal. Usually this move is followed by 2 . . . N–KB3 and 3 . . . P–KN3, and is then called the Pirc Defense. Until the middle 1940's this was thought to be inferior, but now is recognized as a fully satisfactory opening.

1 . . . P–K3

This can be looked upon as analagous to 1 . . . P–QB3. Black plans to challenge White's K4 by 2 . . . P–Q4, thereby also establishing firm control of his Q4 square and exerting pressure on his K5. The diagonals of the KB and Queen are also opened. This is the well–known French Defense. Former World Champion Mikhail Botvinnik was an early adherent of it. Currently the East German Grandmaster Wolfgang Uhlmann plays it exclusively and Grandmasters Viktor Korchnoi and Lajos Portisch have it as part of their repertoire.

1 . . . P–K4

This is just as good as White's first move: it controls K4 and attacks on Q5, while opening the diagonals for the Queen and KB. However, since the pawn is unprotected here, Black will have to endure some pressure on it. Further play is required to determine what opening will result.

1 . . . N–KB3

Strategically logical, as the KN is developed to its preferred square even as it attacks White's KP. Of course, White can chase the Knight away with 2 P–K5 and gain some further time by attacking it again. This defense was originated by World Champion Aleksander Alekhine in the early days of the "hypermodern 1920's" and is therefore named after him. It took some time before its tactical soundness was established. It conclusively established its theoretical soundness when Fischer twice chose it in his 1972 match with Spassky.

1 . . . P–KN3

Black will develop his King–Bishop toward the center with 2 . . . B–N2, while at the same time preparing rapid Kingside castling. Since White is given the opportunity to build up a strong center, Black's plan was long thought to be somewhat dubious. Latest analysis shows that Black can cope with White's initial central superiority, and thus 1 . . . P–KN3 must be rated as perfectly good. However, Black must understand the nuances of this defense very well, as otherwise White's center will smother him. Some writers call this opening "The Modern Defense," but, as such a name will seem ludicrous some years hence, the generic "King's Bishop Fianchetto" or the historical "Robatsch" after the Austrian grandmaster Karl Robatsch seems more appropriate to me.

B) 1 P–Q4

Black also has seven perfect replies here, as shown in Diagram 6:

DIAGRAM 6

BLACK

WHITE

*Black's seven perfect
replies to 1 P–Q4*

1 . . . P–QB3

Preparing to continue with the centrally desirable 2 . . . P–Q4. After 2 P–QB4 P–Q4 Black has selected the Slav Defense of the Queen's Gambit Declined, whereas after 2 P–K4 P–Q4 we have reached, by transposition, the Caro-Kann Defense. Though rarely played, 1 . . . P–QB3, when followed by 2 . . . P–Q4, is a truly perfect move.

1 . . . P–QB4

Black immediately challenges White's QP. After the normal response 2 P–Q5, Black has the choice of playing . . . P–K4 to set up the old Benoni formation or to challenge White's advanced QP with a later . . . P–K3, which leads to the Modern Benoni. In either case White remains with a clear space advantage. Very accurate defense by Black is necessary, yet with it his prospects are O.K.

1 . . . P–Q3

This exerts control on K4 and frees the QB. After 2 P–QB4 N–KB3 King's Indian formations result, and after 2 P–K4 N–KB3 play usually proceeds on Pirc lines (see above). The immediate 1 . . . P–Q3 is unusual, yet fully in accordance with opening principles.

1 . . . P–Q4

With exactly the same point as White's excellent move: controlling Q4, attacking K5, opening the QB's diagonal and preparing the development of the Queen.

1 . . . P–K3

This move controls Q4 and frees both the Queen and KB for action. After 2 P–K4 Black will enter the French Defense with 2 . . . P–Q4, whereas after 2 P–QB4 Black has the choice of bringing about the Queen's Gambit Declined with 2 . . . P–Q4 or of continuing his Kingside development with 2 . . . N–KB3.

1 . . . N–KB3

Black's most flexible reply, and currently the most popular move in tournament play. By developing the KN towards the center, Black furthers every one of his opening objectives.

1 . . . P–KN3

With the same ideas as after 1 P–K4 P–KN3: to fianchetto the KB and to prepare for Kingside castling. After 2 P–QB4 B–N2 the play develops according to the closed QP openings, while after 2 P–K4 B–N2 the more open play characteristic of KP openings results.

C) 1 P–QB4

Again Black has seven perfect replies as shown in Diagram 7:

DIAGRAM 7

BLACK

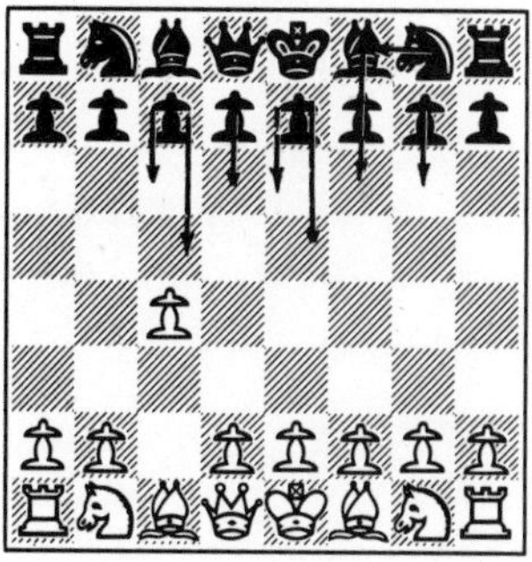

WHITE

*Black's seven perfect
replies to 1 P–QB4*

1 . . . P–QB3

Black plans to challenge White's QBP and establish control of his Q4 via the coming 2 . . . P–Q4. After 2 P–Q4 P–Q4 the Slav Defense results, and 2 P–K4 P–Q4 leads to a less usual variation of the Caro-Kann.

1 . . . P–QB4

Again aping White's logical plan: Black exerts pressure on the centrally important Q4 square, is now ready to develop the QN without disadvantage to its ideal QB3 square, and the Queen is also made available for Queenside play.

1 . . . P–Q3

Guarding K4 and freeing the QB. Black can follow up with 2 . . . P–K4, 2 . . . N–KB3 or 2 . . . P–KN3, depending on his own wishes. Though not common, 1 . . . P–Q3 is fine in all respects.

1 . . . P–K3

Guarding Q4 and freeing the Queen and KB. Black will continue either with 2 . . . P–Q4 or 2 . . . N–KB3.

1 . . . P–K4

An active plan, whereby Black occupies a key central square, attacks White's Q4 and frees his Queen and KB.

1 . . . N–KB3

Again the most flexible response, with all opening objectives being furthered. Black can choose a large number of systems on his second move: 2 . . . P–B3, 2 . . . P–B4, 2 . . . P–K3 and 2 . . . P–KN3.

1 . . . P–KN3

Black immediately shows that he wants to fianchetto his KB. This is a very flexible plan, and, since 1 P–QB4 is not a primary central move, Black doesn't have to worry about White building up an unduly strong center.

D) 1 N–KB3

As shown in Diagram 8, Black has the following seven perfect moves:

1. 1 . . . **P–QB3**
2. 1 . . . **P–QB4**
3. 1 . . . **P–Q3**
4. 1 . . . **P–Q4**
5. 1 . . . **P–K3**
6. 1 . . . **N–KB3**
7. 1 . . . **P–KN3**

These moves have appeared before, and here bestow the same advantages and are justified by the same rationale. Since 1 N–KB3 is not an active thrust, Black has no practical need to prepare . . . P–Q4 by the preliminary 1 . . . P–QB3. However, there is nothing wrong with 1 . . . P–QB3 and often the same position is reached as after 1 . . . P–Q4. For instance, the popular Reti Opening can start 1 N–KB3 P–Q4 2 P–QB4 P–QB3, or alternatively 1 N–KB3 P–QB3 2 P–QB4 P–Q4.

DIAGRAM 8

BLACK

WHITE

*Black's seven perfect
replies to 1 N–KB3*

DIAGRAM 9

BLACK

WHITE

*Black's eight perfect
replies to 1 P–KN3*

E) 1 P–KN3

Since this is White's least active move, every one of Black's
eight possible good moves are feasible. As shown in Diagram 9,
they are:

1. 1 . . . P–QB3
2. 1 . . . P–QB4
3. 1 . . . P–Q3
4. 1 . . . P–Q4
5. 1 . . . P–K3
6. 1 . . . P–K4
7. 1 . . . N–KB3
8. 1 . . . P–KN3

Each of these moves has been discussed earlier in depth, and the same reasoning applies here as well. As the reader has been studying the individual sections, I am sure that he has noticed well before this how the good replies keep repeating themselves. What is good against one opening is also good against a different one, because the same *principles* of opening play apply. The eight perfect Black moves, according to opening principles, are the ones shown above. Unless there is a clear specific reason why it is not playable, you cannot go wrong in choosing one of them no matter what White's first move is.

There is another first move by Black which deserves special mention. In the late 1970's British masters, led by Grandmasters Anthony Miles and Raymond Keene have started playing 1 . . . P–QN3 with generally good success. The idea behind this move is similar to the one behind 1 . . . P–KN3, in that the fianchettoed Bishop will bear down on two primary central squares—in the case of 1 . . . P–QN3 these are Q4 and K5. However, in comparison with 1 . . . P–KN3, 1 . . . P–QN3 has the disadvantage of doing nothing for King safety via castling (castling Queenside is generally inappropriate in these lines). The lack of castling means both that Black's King may remain less secure and that Black's counterplay in the center cannot be supported by his KR. A partial compensation for Black is that his fianchettoed QB can naturally bear down on White's KP in case White plays for a strong center with an early P–K4.

It is still too early to give a definitive answer regarding the objective value of defenses starting with 1 . . . P–QN3. Chess theory, with its endless search for truth, will give its answer in due course. My best guess is that 1 . . . P–QN3 is a bit too passive to be objectively rated as perfect. However, it is in any case no more than a shade worse than the perfect moves. It is possible that after the less active 1 N–KB3, there are no theoretical deficiencies at all in the reply 1 . . . P–QN3.

SECTION 2. Mediocre Moves

With so many perfect moves available for Black, why choose any other? I don't really know, yet there are those who think that they can do better by "taking the opponent out of the book." Moves which have certain positive features and can therefore qualify as "mediocre" are as follows:

A) 1 P–K4

1 . . . N–QB3—The QN is developed to its preferred square, yet this occurs too early. After White's 2 P–Q4 White gets a significant central superiority, no matter whether Black continues with Aron Nimzovitch's 2 . . . P–Q4 or the alternative 2 . . . P–K4.

1 . . . P–Q4—Challenging White's KP is surely logical, yet Black's problem is that after 2 PxP QxP 3 N–QB3 Q–QR4 4 P–Q4, he has lost time with his Queen and the position of White's QP on the fourth rank gives him a clear central superiority. This is, however, a recognized opening and is called the Center Counter in English–speaking countries and the Scandinavian Defense in other parts of the world.

B) 1 P–Q4

1 . . . N–QB3—By playing the QN out too early Black has central difficulties after 2 P–QB4, 2 P–K4 or 2 P–Q5.

1 . . . P–KB4—The Dutch Defense. Black exerts some control over White's K4 and dreams of attacking chances later on against White's Kingside. However, the drawbacks of this move are obvious: development is not furthered and the Kingside is weakened. Unless one is a grandmaster it is extremely easy to land in a strategically hopeless situation on the Black side of the Dutch.

C) 1 P–QB4

Again the two mediocre moves are 1 . . . N–QB3 and 1 . . . P–KB4, and the discussion in part B applies equally well here.

D) 1 N–KB3

The best that can still be said about 1 . . . N–QB3 and 1 . . . P–KB4 is that they are mediocre. Black's QN development could work well if White continues quietly, but if White plays the active 2 P–Q4!, then Black's voluntary obstruction of his QBP again makes it impossible to establish a fully satisfactory central formation.

E) 1 P–KN3

1 . . . P–KB4 again neglects development and weakens the Kingside. Against 1 . . . N–QB3 White should seize his chance for central superiority with 2 P–Q4!. Then the best that Black can achieve are some strategically unsatisfactory variations in the Tschigorin Defense.

Again the reader has no doubt noted how certain patterns of mediocrity repeat themselves. Against closed openings these are the premature development of the QN (although admittedly to its best square) and the centrally helpful yet non-developmental 1 . . . P–KB4. Against 1 P–K4, apart from the QN move, Black can also choose the overly aggressive 1 . . . P–Q4.

SECTION 3. Poor Moves

Moves that were poor for White will be even worse for Black. Therefore never play 1 . . . P–QR3, 1 . . . P–QR4, 1 . . . N–QR3, 1 . . . P–KB3, 1 . . . P–KN4, 1 . . . P–KR3, 1 . . . P–KR4, 1 . . . N–KR3—their White counterparts were poor, and each of them is a bit more than Black can afford.

Two moves do deserve some explanation of why they should be rated as poor rather than mediocre. The first is 1 . . . P–QN4 as a counter to 1 P–Q4, 1 N–KB3 or 1 P–KN3. As the reader will recall, White's P–QN4 on the first move was rated as mediocre. Yet Black, being a move behind, can not afford both to weaken his Queenside and to lose the time necessary to defend the unprotected pawn. For instance, after 1 P–Q4 P–QN4 2 P–K4 B–N2 3 P–KB3 Black has to lose a move in order to protect his QNP.

The other "unplayable" move worth special mention is 1 . . .

P–Q4 as a response to 1 P–QB4. There are two reasons why 1 . . . P–Q4 is worse against 1 P–QB4 than against 1 P–K4:

(1) After 2 PxP, White has exchanged a secondary central pawn (the QBP) for Black's primary central pawn, so that White will be able to build up a considerably stronger center than against the Center Counter Defense. White will have both a QP and KP, whereas Black's only remaining primary central pawn will be the KP.

(2) After the normal moves 2 PxP QxP 3 N–QB3, White will have an edge in development, and also the stronger center after 4 P–Q4. Yet because the position remains relatively closed, Black's opportunities for counterplay are considerably less than in the Center Counter.

CHAPTER 4
Evaluation of Moves: The Practical Approach

On the first move everything is rather clear. If you play in accordance with opening principles, your choice will be fine. But how about on move two or move 10? As the play develops, the position becomes more complicated, and, necessarily, more specific thinking is required when selecting your move. Yet it can not be overemphasized that, on balance, your choices will work out much better if they are supportive of the basic principles. To give preference voluntarily to a move which is nondevelopmental, immaterial for center play and deleterious to King safety is madness unless it also offers some fantastic positive feature(s). In fact, such features exist only rarely. Most moves that are unmindful of opening principles turn out to be clearly inferior. Yet the yen for experimentation often grips chess masters as well as amateurs. Too often we think that perhaps "in this specific position" we can choose a move that violates basic principles, because a special situation exists. Statistics show that such special situations exist much more rarely than we—in our creative optimism—think.

What kind of benchmarks should we use in deciding whether a move is good? By far the best guide is its conformity to good opening principles. It should further at least one of our basic objectives. The kind of thinking to use will be demonstrated in the following examples, illustrating both traditional and new ideas. All the major openings will be considered, with the exception of the Sicilian Defense and the Queen's Gambit, as these will be covered in depth in Chapters 5–8.

Ruy Lopez
Georgiev–Razuvaev, Dubna 1979

1 P–K4 P–K4   2 N–KB3

Developing the KN towards the center with a gain of time is a perfect move and White's best choice here.

2 . . . N–QB3

The KP needs protection, and providing this by developing the QN to its best central location is Black's most popular response. Since Black has selected the KP to be his main central bastion, the use of his QBP for central work is neither required nor readily possible. Therefore there is no disadvantage in the QN's blocking the QBP in this case.

3 B–N5

Completing the development of the minor pieces on the Kingside and preparing to castle immediately. By attacking the QN, White exerts indirect pressure on Black's KP. Thus it can be seen that the Bishop move is actually part of White's plan to achieve central superiority. White's third move has brought about the well–known Ruy Lopez opening.

3 . . . P–QR3

Chasing back the Bishop, since White can't win a pawn by 4 BxN QPxB! 5 NxP?! because of 5 . . . Q–Q5, and Black regains the pawn with a fine game. However, it is not at all obvious that 3 . . . P–QR3 is a good move, and it required extensive tests in master games before the value of the move was established.

4 B–R4

Maintaining the status quo. An alternate plan of equivalent value is 4 BxN QPxB   5 0–0!.

4 . . . N–B3

Developing the KN to its best central square.

5 0–0

And so in five moves White has achieved good central pressure and development while bringing his King to safety by castling.

White has no need to fear 5 . . . NxP since after 6 P–Q4! he will win back the pawn by force. Though not completely obvious, this conclusion can be anticipated because the open nature of the position will require Black to concern himself with the safety of his own King. Therefore, he will also have to castle rapidly, and White will be able to capture Black's KP while the latter is catching up in development.

5 . . . P–QN4

A controversial move. To prevent threats to his KP, Black protects his QN from attack by White's Bishop but chases it onto the diagonal aiming at Black's KB2. Unless Black can castle rapidly, this square can become very vulnerable. The time tested, most common, move is the quietly developmental 5 . . . B–K2.

6 B–N3 B–K2   7 R–K1

By protecting the KP with his Rook, White brings about the normal position in the Closed Ruy Lopez, which usually results after 5 . . . B–K2   6 R–K1 P–QN4   7 B–N3. Instead, White can force Black to solve more difficult problems with the aggressive 7 P–Q4!, since after 7 . . . PxP   8 P–K5 is very annoying.

Note that after 7 R–K1 White's Rook is centrally placed. At the moment its primary function is defensive, but it can also readily become aggressive along the King–file.

7 . . . 0–0

Black's King is now safe.

8 P–B3

Planning to build a strong center with 9 P–Q4.

8 . . . P–Q3

Protecting the KP and opening up the diagonal of the QB. If White proceeds with the immediate 9 P–Q4, Black can exert strong pressure on the QP with 9 . . . B–N5.

9 P–KR3!

The sole purpose of this move is to be able to play P–Q4 without allowing the pin. Since Black cannot prevent the coming P–Q4, nor has any immediate threat, White can afford this loss of time. The position after White's 9th move has been analyzed to great depth, since Black has many possibilities. Formerly the Tschigorin Variation (9 . . . N–QR4   10 B–B2 P–B4) was very common, and in the 1970's Breyer's idea of 9 . . . N–N1   10 P–Q4 QN–Q2 caught fire.

9 . . . B–N2!?

Only in the last couple of years has this move appeared in master practice. Why has it taken so long for this discovery to be made? Based on basic opening principles, the move is surely worth very serious investigation. Black completes the development of his minor pieces and positions the QB directly on the center. Whenever Black's QN moves away, the Bishop will be bearing down on White's KP.

10 P–Q4 R–K1

DIAGRAM 10

BLACK

WHITE

Ruy Lopez
Georgiev–Razuvaev
Dubna 1979
after Black's 10th move

The basic position in this sub-variation. Black's Rook is posted both to support his KP and indirectly to attack White's KP. Since White has some central superiority, he still has the slight advantage that comes with his right to make the first move. His most consistent plan now is to start developing the Queenside pieces with 11 QN–Q2. Instead, White shows that he is satisfied to draw against his better-known opponent. The Soviet grandmaster playing Black is not satisfied with such a result. However, by continuing the game with second rate moves, he avoids the draw only to lose instead: 11 N–N5 R–KB1 12 N–B3 P–R3?! 13 QN–Q2 PxP?! 14 PxP N–QN5 15 Q–K2 P–B4 16 P–R3 N–B3 17 PxP PxP 18 P–K5 N–R2 19 N–K4 P–B5 20 B–B2 R–K1?! 21 B–B4! N–B1 22 Q–K3 N–N3 23 P–K6! NxB 24 PxPch KxP 25 QxNch K–N1 26 Q–B5! R–KB1 27 Q–K6ch R–B2 28 QR–Q1 Q–QB1 29 Q–N6 RxN 30 N–Q6! BxN 31 RxB K–B1 32 PxR Q–B2 33 R/6–K6 Q–B2 34 QxQch KxQ 35 B–N6ch Black resigns.

Alekhine's Defense
Speelman–Suba, Hastings 1978/79

1 P–K4 N–KB3 2 P–K5

The challenged pawn must return the challenge, since allowing the KN to maintain its present post allows Black easy development.

2 . . . N–Q4 3 N–KB3

Developing the KN can't be bad. Even so, the central 3 P–Q4 is at least equally good and considerably more flexible. Then after 3 . . . P–Q3 White can choose, for instance, the very sharp Four Pawns Attack with 4 P–QB4 N–N3 5 P–B4, or the sound, strategic 4 N–KB3.

3 . . . P–Q3

Opening lines for development while at the same time challenging White's outpost is the only logical plan.

4 B–B4

A reasonable spot for the Bishop, yet it really is too soon to tell whether it is the *best* one. The normal, flexible 4 P–Q4! is better suited to retaining an advantage.

4 . . . P–QB3

Keeping the Knight in the center without blocking off the QB's diagonal, as would occur in case of 4 . . . P–K3.

5 N–B3?!

Developing the QN to its best square runs the risk of incurring doubled pawns. Since nothing is gained in return, the plan is dubious. Again White's best is the simple 5 P–Q4.

5 . . . NxN   6 NPxN

Capturing this way enhances White's central pawn prospects; the opposite would be true after capturing away from the center by 6 QPxN?!.

6 . . . P–Q4!

A strategically logical change of plans by Black. White was willing to accept doubled pawns in the hope that the superior development of his minor pieces would yield full compensation. Therefore, Black chooses to close the position, so that he can complete his development without allowing White to undertake anything immediate. Once Black's development is complete he can start to exploit White's structural weakness—the doubled QBPs.

7 B–K2 B–N5!

Black needs to play . . . P–K3 to develop the KB, yet doing so on move seven would lock in the QB. Therefore Black develops it first.

8 R–QN1 Q–B2   9 P–Q4 P–K3   10 0–0 N–Q2   11 P–KR3 BxN

Since Black's pawn formation does not harmonize well with his light-squared Bishop, and since the position is rather blocked, Black is fully justified in this exchange. However, 11 . . . B–R4 is also O.K.

12 BxB 0–0–0

Black's King is safe, his position has no structual weaknesses, and he can develop the KB at his leisure. White has no compensation for his immobile QBPs. On the whole Black's prospects are slightly better. In further play Black obtained a winning position, but his error on Move 33 allowed White to salvage a draw: 13 Q–Q3 N–N3! 14 B–K2 K–N1 15 B–N5 R–B1 16 R–N3 P–KR3 17 B–R4? P–QB4! 18 PxP N–Q2 19 R–N2 NxBP 20 Q–Q4 P–KN4 21 B–N3 N–K5 22 KR–N1 NxB! 23 B–R6 P–N3 24 RxPch PxR

DIAGRAM 11

BLACK

WHITE

Alekhine's Defense
Speelman–Suba
Hastings 1978/79
after Black's 12th move

25 RxPch K–R1 26 B–N5 Q–R2! 27 R–R6 B–B4 28 RxQch BxR
29 Q–QR4 R–B2 30 B–B6ch K–N1 31 Q–N5ch K–B1 32
Q–R6ch K–Q1 33 BxP! R–K1? (The winning method is 33 . . .
PxB! 34 Q–B6ch K–Q2 35 QxR N–K5 36 Q–KB8 BxPch 37
K–B1 K–K3, as given by Suba) 34 B–B6 N–K7ch 35 K–B1 NxP
36 Q–Q3ch N–Q4 37 P–QB4! RxB 38 PxN R–B8ch 39 K–K2
PxP 40 QxPch K–B1 41 Q–R8ch B–N1 42 Q–R6ch K–Q2 43
Q–Q3ch! K–B2 44 Q–Q6ch Draw.

French Defense
Sznapik–Hort, Helsinki 1979

1 P–K4 P–K3 2 P–Q4 P–Q4

The basic position in the French Defense. White's KP is
challenged, and it must either move or be protected. It is easy to
see that 3 PxP PxP! allows complete symmetry and equality.

3 N–Q2

The best way of protecting the pawn is with the QN. For this
purpose 3 N–QB3 looks ideal, but after that move Black can apply

an annoying pin with 3 . . . B–N5. Therefore currently the text move—originally championed by the great German player Siegbert Tarrasch—is very popular. White prevents the potential pin and keeps the QBP free for central action. However, there also are two negative aspects: the diagonal of the QB is now blocked, and the Knight exerts less pressure on the center (i.e., on the important Q5 square).

3 . . . N–KB3

Developing the KN with a gain of time by attacking the KP is a good logical plan. Theoretically playable, though strategically somewhat inconsistent is immediately to give up the fight for the center by playing 3 . . . PxP. After 4 NxP White's QP controls more central space than Black's KP, while Black's QB remains blocked. A perfectly good alternative, however, is 3 . . . P–QB4, whereby Black tries to take advantage of the less active location of White's QN by posing a direct challenge to both of White's central pawns.

4 P–K5

Still harmless is 4 PxP PxP. Since there is no fully satisfactory way of keeping the KP protected, White advances it with a gain of time.

4 . . . KN–Q2

The best response. Instead, 4 . . . N–N1 is a clear loss of time, whereas 4 . . . N–K5 risks having a vulnerable doubled pawn after 5 NxN.

5 P–QB3

Since Black will be attacking the QP—the base of White's central pawn chain—by means of an imminent . . . P–QB4, White reinforces it. Of equivalent value are the developmental 5 B–Q3 or 5 P–KB4, supporting the KP.

5 . . . P–QB4

Note how the dynamics of Black's counterplay against the White center alter as the situation warrants. First he applies pressure to White's KP, and then, when this pawn is stabilized, Black switches over to attack the QP.

6 B–Q3

It must be logical to place the Bishop on a diagonal where it both helps to influence the center and aims at Black's Kingside. A strong alternative is 6 P–KB4. At the cost of one tempo he might otherwise have spent developing his pieces White reinforces control of the key K5 square and is prepared in certain situations to advance against Black's Kingside with P–KB5.

6 . . . P–QN3

Since the central pawn formation of the French allows White's light-colored Bishop much more scope than the corresponding Black Bishop, Black prepares to exchange his Bishop after the coming . . . B–QR3. This idea is based on sound strategic principles. Its disadvantage is that it costs considerable time in a position where White already has a nice space advantage. The most usual move for Black is the consistent, developmental 6 . . . N–QB3, bringing the QN to its ideal square while attacking the QP.

7 N–K2

There is no smooth way of preventing Black's planned . . . B–QR3, so White does best to complete the development of his minor pieces. Then, if White so chooses, he can castle early.

But where should the KN go? Developing it to K2 allows it to head for KB4 or KN3; White can then follow this with a Queen move (most probably Q–N4) directed against Black's Kingside. Additionally, the KBP can be utilized in the coming play. Thus the text move is quite good. Attractive, but less effective, is 7 KN–B3, since White then will have great difficulties in formulating an attack against Black's Kingside, and in the French Defense the Kingside is where White's prospects most often lie. According to the latest theory, however, White's strongest move is the anticentral 7 N–R3!. Of course, this is an exception to the principle that the pieces should be developed toward the center. The specific strengths of the move are:

(1) The Knight can get to both KB4 and KN5—the two most useful attacking locations for the Knight.

(2) The diagonal Q1–KR5 remains open for White's Queen, and it can therefore easily reach the attacking squares KN4 or KR5.

(3) The KN is developed so that White can castle immediately.

(4) After castling, P–KB4 becomes quite feasible, with the plan of attacking Black's Kingside by means of an eventual P–KB5.

7 . . . B–R3   8 B–N1?!

That White does not want to exchange his "good" Bishop is understandable, yet this retreat both costs time and hands over a nice diagonal to Black's Bishop. Correct is 8 BxB NxB   9 0–0, and White's spatial advantage plus edge in development gives him the better chances.

8 . . . N–QB3

Developing while at the same time threatening to win the QP.

9 N–B3 P–QN4?

The sortie with the QNP costs two tempos while accomplishing nothing positive. Correct is either the developmental 9 . . . B–K2 or 9 . . . PxP, opening the Queenside. In either case Black has approximate equality.

10 0–0 P–N5   11 R–K1!

White has castled, substantially completed his development, and retained his clear central superiority. Black has no coherent way of coping with White's spatial and developmental advantages. Although he is a world class player, Black is now decisively defeated: 11 . . . BxN   12 QxB PxQP   13 PxQP Q–N3   14 B–K3 B–K2   15 B–Q3 R–QB1   16 QR–B1 R–B2   17 P–KR4! P–KR4   18 B–QN5! P–N3   19 BxN RxB   20 RxR QxR   21 R–QB1 Q–N2   22 B–N5! BxB   23 NxB K–K2   24 Q–B3 R–KB1   25 Q–B4 P–B4   26 Q–Q2! R–QN1   27 N–R3! N–B1   28 R–B5 N–Q2   29 R–B2 N–B1   30 K–R2 K–K1   31 Q–B1 K–Q2   32 Q–R6 K–K1   33 N–B4 Q–KB2   34 N–Q3! Q–K2   35 P–KN3 P–N6   36 PxP K–B2   37 N–B4 K–N1

DIAGRAM 12

BLACK

WHITE

French Defense
Sznapik-Hort
Helsinki 1979
after White's 11th move

38 NxNP Q–KN2　39 QxQch KxQ　40 N–B4! RxP and Black resigned without awaiting White's reply.

Queen's Indian Defense
Unzicker–Korchnoi, South Africa 1979

1 P–Q4 N–KB3　2 P–QB4

By far the most active central move. The QBP bears on the important Q5 square, and the QN can be developed at White's leisure to its ideal location at QB3. In addition, the Queen can now be developed toward the Queenside.

2 . . . P–K3

Acting on the key Q4 square and allowing the development of the KB. After the latter is accomplished, Black will be able to castle.

3 N–KB3

One of the two best and most popular moves. The KN is developed to its ideal central square and the way prepared for Kingside castling.

The alternative is 3 N–QB3, which is thought to be a bit sharper, since it "threatens" the strong central advance 4 P–K4. A large number of players currently do not play 3 N–QB3 because they prefer not to allow 3 . . . B–N5, pinning the Knight and establishing the Nimzo–Indian Defense.

3 . . . P–QN3

This is the move characteristic of the Queen's Indian Defense. Black will fianchetto his QB (to fianchetto means to place a Bishop on QN2 or KN2) and thereby exert strong pressure on Q4 and particularly K5. However, Black also has three other logical plans: (1) 3 . . . P–Q4, transposing into the Queen's Gambit Declined (see Chapter 7), (2) 3 . . . P–B4, challenging the QP and, after 4 P–Q5 PxP 5 PxP P–Q3, reaching the Modern Benoni Defense, and (3) 3 . . . B–N5ch, offering to trade off the Bishop and achieve rapid castling.

4 P–KN3

White fianchettos his KB to oppose Black's on the central diagonal. This is by far the most popular move. Also good and in accordance with opening principles are 4 N–B3 and 4 P–K3.

4 . . . B–R3!?

But what is this? Has Black lost his senses? Wasn't the point of 3 . . . P–QN3 to continue 4 . . . B–N2? The answer is yes: 4 . . . B–N2 is in fact the normal response and leads to the main line of the Queen's Indian.

Nevertheless, the eccentric–looking text move has an important point, and therefore has shown itself to be a satisfactory alternative to 4 . . . B–N2. From the QR3 square the Bishop attacks the QBP, and White's most efficient response is 5 P–K3. Yet coming on the heels of 4 P–KN3, 5 P–K3? would lead to a noticeable weakening of the light squares on the Kingside, since White could no longer fianchetto the KB while it is needed to protect the QBP. As will be seen shortly, all other methods of protecting this pawn also have sufficient shortcomings to allow Black good chances for ultimate equality.

5 Q–R4

Protecting the QBP while applying pressure against Black's Queenside. This is White's most usual move. However, the Queen is somewhat exposed here and no longer exerts much influence on the center. Still, there is nothing better. After either 5 Q–B2 or 5 QN–Q2, Black effectively challenges White's QP with 5 . . . P–B4!, since the response 6 P–Q5 is now impossible. After 5 P–N3, Black gets good counterplay with 5 . . . B–N5ch! 6 B–Q2 B–K2! 7 B–N2 P–B3! 8 0–0 P–Q4.

5 . . . N–K5?!

A new and interesting idea, yet too eccentric to be fully satisfactory. Black tries to exploit the awkward position of White's Queen, but moving an already developed piece twice more, loses far too much time. After the indicated 5 . . . P–B4 or 5 . . . P–B3 Black's prospects for equality are bright.

6 B–N2 N–Q3   7 P–B5!

Active play is required to take advantage of White's momentary edge in development. Harmless is 7 KN–Q2?! P–QB3 8 Q–B2 N–B4 9 N–KB3 P–Q4 10 PxP BPxP with Black at least equal in Trois–Tarjan, Riga Interzonal 1979.

7 . . . PxP

7 . . . N–N2 8 P–QN4 gives White a powerful bind on the Queenside.

8 PxP N–N2   9 P–B6!

At the cost of a doubled pawn, White destroys Black's counterplay and completes his own development efficiently. Since White will exert pressure along the QB file against Black's pawns, he has every expectation of at the least recovering his investment.

9 . . . PxP   10 N–B3! B–Q3   11 0–0 0–0   12 R–Q1

Note how consistently all of White's pieces have been developed towards the center. Black's pieces, on the other hand, particularly his Knights, stand awkwardly rather than usefully. White's advantage, though not large, is both pleasant and free of risk. The game continued: 12 . . . Q–K1   13 N–Q4 N–Q1   14 B–K3 B–N2

DIAGRAM 13

BLACK

WHITE

Queen's Indian Defense
Unzicker–Korchnoi
South Africa 1979
after White's 12th move

15 N–N3 N–Q2   16 N–K4 N–N3   17 Q–R5 P–KB4, and now instead of 18 N/K–B5? which led to less nothing after 18 . . . B–B1 (White still won when Black, in an equal position, overstepped the time limit on move 56), Unzicker suggests the straightforward 18 NxB PxN   19 BxN PxB   20 QxP Q–K2   21 N–R5 R–R3   22 Q–N4 P–B4   23 Q–N5. The more active position, absence of weaknesses, and potential benefit from the passed QRP—all mean that White's opening advantage has been carried through into the middlegame. Note also how effortlessly White recovered the pawn sacrificed on move nine.

English Opening
Timman–Romanishin, Amsterdam 1978

1 P–QB4 P–K4   2 N–QB3 N–KB3   3 N–B3 N–B3

The play so far is clear and sound by both sides: each has pawn presence in the center and has developed the Knights to their ideal squares.

4 P–K3

With the idea of establishing a strong center with 5 P–Q4 by enabling the KP to recapture on Q4, if White so desires. Black should either strive for complications while developing the KB with 4 . . . B–N5 or select the modest, developing 4 . . . B–K2, a plan which Karpov has used successfully.

4 . . . Q–K2?!

A novelty. By pinning White's KP, Black prevents it from recapturing on Q4. However, the cost in time, the anti-developmental consequence of having the Queen blockade the KB, and the fact that the Queen is not well placed on K2—all this suggests that Black's plan can hardly succeed.

5 P–Q4! PxP   6 NxP

Even though White has had to capture with the KN, the consequences of the respective fourth moves are clear: White is ahead in development and has superiority in the center, while the position of the Black Queen makes it difficult for Black to complete his Kingside development.

6 . . . P–KN3?!

It is logical for Black to want to fianchetto the KB, but this move allows a nasty attack on the QBP. Therefore, 6 . . . P–Q3 first was correct.

7 N/4–N5!

Usually in such closed openings, the prospects for successful cavalry charges so early in the game are slight. Yet the clumsy location of Black's Queen and White's edge in development change the normal odds.

7 . . . P–Q3   8 N–Q5! NxN   9 PxN N–K4   10 P–B4!

White now has an undisputed central superiority. With his 11th move he extends his existing edge in development by a further gain of time.

10 . . . N–N5   11 B–K2 N–B3   12 Q–R4!

White's spatial advantage and superior development, coupled with the Black King's inability to castle, puts Black in a most

DIAGRAM 14

BLACK

WHITE

*English Opening
Timman–Romanishin
Amsterdam 1978
after White's 12th move*

unpleasant situation. If now 12 . . . B–Q2, 13 Q–B4! leaves Black in a quandry, and 12 . . . P–B3 13 PxP PxP 14 N–Q4 B–Q2 15 NxP yields White a pawn and the superior position. Black therefore chooses an endgame where his "only" disadvantage is a missing pawn: 12 . . . K–Q1 13 NxRP! (with the threat 14 N–B6ch) 13 . . . Q–K5!? 14 QxQ NxQ 15 NxB KxN 16 B–Q3 N–B4 17 B–B2 B–N2 18 P–QR3 R–K1 19 K–K2 N–R5 20 R–QN1 N–N3 21 R–Q1 R–R4 22 B–N3 P–KB4 23 B–Q2 R–QR1. Black of course has no compensation for the pawn and White won on move 75.

Reti Opening
Stean–Ljubojevic, São Paulo 1979

1 N–KB3 N–KB3   2 P–KN3

White plans to complete his Kingside development and only then look for an active plan.

2 . . . P–QN4!?

Black also wants to contest the light–squared central diagonal and thus prepares to fianchetto the QB. He thrusts the QNP two

squares forward in order to control White's QB4 square. The pawn
is somewhat weak here, yet because White, with 2 P–KN3, has
effectively relinquished his option to attack it with his KB (since
the Bishop now belongs on KN2 rather than on the KB1–QR6
diagonal), Black can just get away with his aggressiveness.

3 B–N2 B–N2 4 0–0

In just four moves White has gotten his King to safety, developed
his KN and KB towards the center and prepared for concrete
action.

4 . . . P–B4

Grabbing more space in the center and on the Queen's side.

5 P–Q3

White's first central pawn move, controlling the primary K4 and
secondary QB4 squares and allowing development of the QB.

5 . . . N–B3

Continuing the development of his Queenside forces. Black so
far has been able to neglect his Kingside development because
White is not aiming for any kind of a direct attack against his King.

6 P–K4

The first active central move. White is now ready to continue
with P–K5, and so Black prevents it in the most normal manner.

6 . . . P–Q3 7 N–B3

Developing the QN with a gain of time. Advancing the QNP
further is no particular gain for Black since White will then be able
to start undermining it.

7 . . . P–N5 8 N–Q5! N–Q2!

Black needs to chase White's QN back with a gain of time. Inferior are both 8 . . . NxN?! 9 PxN, with White having a
developmental and spatial advantage, and 8 . . . P–K3?! 9 NxNch
QxN 10 P–B3!, with White again ahead in development and
Black's Queen clumsily placed.

9 P–B3 P–K3   10 N–B4

Stean considers 10 N–K3! to be more accurate in view of the forthcoming play in the center.

10 . . . PxP   11 PxP N/3–K4!   12 P–Q4

DIAGRAM 15

BLACK

WHITE

Reti Opening
Stean–Ljubojevic
Sao Paulo 1979
after White's 12th move

This position is slightly in White's favor. He is better developed and has more central space. However, Black has no fundamental weaknesses, and, with the coming exchange of a pair of Knights, his defensive burden is decreased. Black's play must be accurate to hold on, and in the game he achieved ultimate equality as follows: 12 . . . NxNch   13 BxN B–K2   14 R–N1 R–QN1   15 P–Q5 P–K4 16 N–N2 B–R3   17 RxR QxR   18 B–K2 BxB   19 QxB 0–0   20 N–K3 P–N3   21 Q–R6 P–B4!   22 Q–Q3 PxP!   23 QxP N–B3   24 Q–QR4 Draw.

KB Fianchetto Opening
Seirawan–Miles, Lone Pine 1979

1 P–KN3 P–K4

An active, perfectly good response.

2 P–QB4

After the immediate 2 B–N2, Black could occupy the center with 2 . . . P–Q4. Therefore White establishes a direct pawn presence himself and only afterwards will continue with the planned development of the Kingside.

2 . . . P–QB3

A very demanding approach. Black is determined to enforce . . . P–Q4. He already has good central presence, thanks to his KP, yet is determined to have a lot more. This is a very double–edged plan, because White—with the advantage of the first move—will be able to start undermining Black's imposing–looking center very quickly.

3 B–N2 P–Q4   4 PxP PxP   5 P–Q4!

White establishes his own strong central presence while challenging Black's KP. Clearly unsatisfactory now is 5 . . . PxP?!, because after 6 N–KB3 White will effortlessly recapture the pawn and Black's isolated QP will remain a chronic weakness.

5 . . . P–K5   6 P–B3!

Again challenging the KP. Throughout, White gives a classic demonstration of how to cope with and undermine prematurely advanced center pawns. If now 6 . . . PxP?!, then 7 NxP, and White's KN has landed on its ideal square with a gain of time while Black's isolated QP will remain a chronic weakness.

6 . . . P–B4

The bastion in the center must be held. Yet there also are disadvantages to this natural move: Black's Kingside is weakened, as are the dark squares (in particular K4), and the QB's scope is decreased.

7 N–KR3!

Remember that White's immediate strategic plan is to complete the development of his Kingside. The only square available for the

KN is KR3, and it is not a bad one in this case because the Knight will be able to go on to KB4.

7 . . . N–QB3

Normal and good.

8 0–0 B–K2   9 N–B3

Developing the QN to its ideal square, from where it will be able to pressure Black's QP.

9 . . . N–B3   10 B–N5!

Completing the development of the minor pieces and indirectly applying pressure on the QP. If now 10 . . . 0–0?!, then 11 N–B4!, and Black's QP is in mortal danger. Therefore he must bring up his QB to help defend his center.

10 . . . B–K3   11 N–B4

Developing the momentarily wayward KN towards the center with a gain of time.

11 . . . B–B2   12 P–K3

White's QP also needs support and this is the simplest and best way of providing it.

12 . . . 0–0

And so Black has brought his King to safety by castling, the minor pieces are developed and his central influence seems secure. Nevertheless, White's next move points up the weakness in Black's camp:

13 PxP!

Black's problem is that he has no good way of recapturing *in order to retain his central* influence. As a matter of fact, the lesser evil here is 13 . . . NxKP! 14 BxB NxB, though White's more active position and the weaknesses of Black's QP and dark squares do give White a steady plus. Inferior is 13 . . . BPxP?! because of 14 B–R3! Q–Q3   15 N–N5 Q–Q1   16 N–K6 BxN   17 BxBch K–R1 18 B–B4 N–K1   19 Q–R5 P–QR3   20 N–B3 N–B3   21 Q–R3, with White's forces applying very strong pressure on Black's position.

DIAGRAM 16

BLACK

WHITE

KB Fianchetto Opening
Seirawan–Miles
Lone Pine 1979
after White's 13th move

Also inferior is the game's 13 . . . QPxP?! because it not only yields White an immediate passed protected QP, but, even more importantly, Black's center pawns remain vulnerable to a further successful undermining. White realized his advantages in the following exemplary fashion: 13 . . . QPxP?! 14 B–R3 P–KN3 15 P–KN4! PxP 16 BxN! PxB 17 BxB QxB 18 Q–N4 B–B5 19 R–B2 R–B4 20 NxRP R–KR4 21 R–N2! R–R5 22 Q–N3 R–KB1 23 N–KN5 R–R4 24 P–N3! B–Q6 25 N–Q5 Q–Q2 26 N–B4 R–R3 27 R–Q1 R–B4 28 P–KR4 NxP (Desperation in a lost position.) 29 PxN QxPch 30 K–R2 Q–K4 31 N/5–R3 Q–B3 32 P–R5 B–N4 33 R/N–Q2 P–N4 34 R–Q5! RxR 35 RxR Q–N7ch 36 N–N2 RxP 37 RxB Black resigns.

CHAPTER 5
Sicilian Defense: Basic Principles

SECTION 1. Introduction

Of all of Black's responses to 1 P–K4, by far the most popular in master chess is 1 . . . P–QB4, called the Sicilian Defense. Its popularity is based on both fundamental and psychological factors. The Sicilian was Robert J. Fischer's primary (and almost exclusive) weapon against the KP from the time he excited the chess world by winning the 1957/58 U.S. Championship at the age of 14 up to the 1972 World Championship match against Boris Spassky. The chess world admired Fischer's successes and great fighting spirit. Since the Sicilian Defense was so intimately associated with Bobby, his admirers felt that there must be something good and, indeed, almost magical about it. Many of the young, upcoming masters started playing it, and in due course this led to significant new discoveries in the theory of this defense, which in turn further enhanced its reputation and therefore its popularity. Currently, at least half of the games starting with 1 P–K4 turn out to be Sicilians.

Let us look again at the basic starting point as shown in Diagram 17.

The reasons for playing the Sicilian and the strategic ideas behind it are:

1. Black's 1 . . . P–QB4 is so dissimilar to White's 1 P–K4 that, invariably, very unbalanced positions result. In competitive chess this greatly increases Black's practical winning chances.

DIAGRAM 17

BLACK

WHITE

Sicilian Defense
1 P–K4 P–QB4

When a master needs to win with Black, his natural opening choice is the Sicilian. In the later stages of his 1972 match with Fischer, when he was far behind and needed to win, Spassky turned exclusively to the Sicilian even though it was not a primary part of his opening repertoire.

2. Black's immediate central emphasis is on White's Q4 square, and, if White foregoes playing P–Q4 (as for instance in the various "closed" variations), then Black's control over this square continues.

3. Since 1 . . . P–QB4 establishes a beachhead on the Queenside, Black's opportunities for active play are generally on that side.

4. In normal variations White plays an early P–Q4—usually on the third move. After Black exchanges pawns with . . . PxP, the QB file is then half open, and this file becomes Black's primary attacking route on the Queenside.

5. White's KP is strongly placed on the fourth rank. If Black can get in . . . P–Q4 to eliminate White's KP *with no resultant disadvantages,* he obtains full equality. Therefore, aiming for . . . P–Q4 becomes Black's chief strategic objective; however, to achieve it early in the game is rarely possible.

Of course, 1 . . . P–QB4 also entails some disadvantages—otherwise it would be the only opening played! These disadvantages are:

1. Black ignores White's very strong and active pawn on K4, enabling White to build up strong attacking chances on the Kingside.

2. 1 . . . P–QB4 is not really a primary developing move. The only piece whose development it furthers immediately is the Queen. It contributes nothing towards the development of the Kingside, the area where White is anticipated to attack.

3. By allowing White to set up a strong attacking formation on the Kingside, Black risks succumbing to a sudden mating assault. In the early stages of the game Black is in considerably greater practical danger than White, since an attack on the King can be decisive far more quickly than an attack against a Queenside point.

In general, White tries for an attack on the Kingside in the Sicilian and Black for one on the Queenside. Black must both parry White's attack and create counterplay for himself on the Queenside. If he is successful, he has good chances of winning any endgame that results. White has good prospects of scoring with an early Kingside attack.

It must be emphasized that, even though it is fully sound theoretically, the Sicilian Defense is difficult to handle in practical play. A bit of carelessness in defending—and the King goes lost! It is actually much better suited for a Fischer than for his many imitators and followers. Nevertheless, it is a very important opening, and I shall try to present its principles as clearly as possible so that the reader, using his brave heart and the information gleaned from this book, can successfully navigate its invariably muddy waters.

Section 2. Basic Principles

The main moves and their significant alternatives are as follows:

1 P–K4 P–QB4 2 N–KB3

The KN is developed to its preferred central location, furthering prospects for early castling and preparing the active and developmental P–Q4. Note that in developing the Kingside minor pieces, it is more effective to develop the KN first and only then the KB. There is a rule of thumb, valid most of the time (including here) that says "Knights should be developed before Bishops." It is easy to understand its application to our second move. The KN's best square is KB3, and there is absolutely no disadvantage in playing it there on the second move. On the other hand, the best location for the KB is as yet uncertain. Depending on Black's play—and one's own taste—it could belong on K2, Q3, QB4 or QN5. Move two is too early to tell.

By any standard of chess evaluation 2 N–KB3 is a perfect move. It is the most popular move, and in master chess is played more than 75% of the time. Thus it follows that in almost one quarter of the games, something else is chosen. These alternatives can be divided into the categories of secondary alternatives and primary alternatives.

The fairly long list of *secondary* alternatives are:

2 P–QN3—White plans to fianchetto his QB to bear down on the central diagonal QR1–KR8. This kind of a strategic approach does not mix well with the immediate activity visualized by 1 P–K4, and Black equalizes with normal sound play, starting with either 2 . . . N–QB3, 2 . . . P–Q3 or 2 . . . P–K3.

2 P–QN4—The so-called Wing Gambit, whereby White takes drastic measures to eliminate Black's QBP. Black should capture 2 . . . PxP, and then, after either 3 P–QR3 or 3 P–Q4, respond with the central advance 3 . . . P–Q4!. This way Black achieves full equality.

2 P–QB4—White pays primary attention to preventing Black's potential . . . P–Q4 advance and is willing to lock in his KB and weaken control of his Q4 square in order to do so. The resulting positions often occur also in the English Opening when White follows 1 P–QB4 with an early P–K4. Black's most effective plan is to grab what White has voluntarily given up: control of White's Q4. Consistent development now would be: 2 . . . N–QB3 3 N–QB3 P–KN3 4 P–KN3 B–N2 5 B–N2 P–Q3 6 P–Q3 N–B3 7 KN–K2 0–0 8 0–0, and now 8 . . . N–K1! both to control Q5 and to have the option of countering White's Kingside play with a timely . . . P–KB4.

2 P–Q3—White shows his interest in a "closed" formation, but this move generally has no independent significance and leads to the positions considered after 2 N–QB3.

2 P–KB4—Prior to playing N–KB3, White advances his KBP both to control K5 and to be in position for later activity along the KB file. However, this move does nothing to further development and weakens the Kingside. Black's most effective plan is to aim for the liberating . . . P–Q4, either after the preparatory 2 . . . P–K3 or immediately (2 . . . P–Q4). Then, after 3 PxP QxP 4 N–QB3 Q–Q1 5 N–B3 N–KB3, Black has approximate equality, because as a result of 2 P–KB4 White is a tempo behind in development and his KBP is somewhat weak.

2 P–KN3—White aims for the immediate fianchetto of his KB, but the lack of attention paid to Black's Q4 square allows Black the immediate 2 . . . P–Q4!. After 3 PxP QxP 4 N–KB3 B–N5! 5 B–N2 Q–K3ch 6 K–B1 the uncastled location of White's King gives Black fully equal counterchances.

2 N–K2—An awkward looking move, yet perfectly playable if White intends to follow up with an early P–Q4. There simply is no way that Black can immediately exploit the Knight's location. Inferior now is 2 . . . N–KB3 3 QN–B3 P–Q4?!, because after 4 PxP NxP 5 NxN QxN 6 P–Q4! PxP 7 QxP QxQ 8 NxQ White's edge in development gives him a significant initiative.

2 B–B4—It is premature to place the Bishop here, since after 2 . . . P–K3!, not only is its anticipated diagonal action inhibited, but after . . . P–Q4 White will have to lose a tempo (one unit of time) in moving it again.

There are three *primary* alternatives to 2 N–KB3:

2 P–QB3—With the logical idea of building a strong center after 3 P–Q4 PxP 4 PxP. Black can try to build his own center with 2 . . . P–K3 3 P–Q4 P–Q4, though he must then accept an isolated QP on 4 KPxP KPxP, since here 4 . . . QxP?! allows White too strong a central influence after 5 N–B3. Or Black can aim to challenge White's center by 2 . . . N–KB3 3 P–K5 N–Q4 4 P–Q4 PxP 5 PxP P–Q3 6 N–KB3 N–QB3. In either case, with careful play Black can be expected to equalize.

2 P–Q4—Leads to the Smith–Morra Gambit after 2 . . . PxP 3 P–QB3 PxP 4 NxP. Theoretically, this gambit is not quite sound since for his pawn White only gains the equivalent of one developmental move. However, in a practical game unwary opponents can go quickly under. Black's most effective plan is to combine central influence with rapid Kingside castling. The suggested approach is: 4 . . . N–QB3 5 N–B3 P–Q3 6 B–QB4 P–K3! 7 0–0 B–K2 8 Q–K2 N–B3 9 R–Q1 P–K4! (Planning 10 . . . B–N5, which would then threaten 11 . . . N–Q5.) 10 P–KR3 0–0. Black then will complete the development of his minor pieces via 11 . . . B–K3! no matter whether White plays 11 B–K3 or 11 B–KN5. Black's position then is sound and solid, and White has to prove he has some compensation for the sacrificed pawn.

2 N–QB3—This can transpose back into the main lines, but its independent significance can be seen after the further moves 2 . . . N–QB3 3 P–KN3 P–KN3 4 B–N2 B–N2 5 P–Q3 P–Q3.

DIAGRAM 18

BLACK

WHITE

Sicilian Defense
Closed Variation
after Black's 5th move

This is the basic starting point of the Closed Variation. Note how White, by choosing a move order starting with 2 N–QB3, has prevented Black's . . . P–Q4. Despite the closed, innocuous appearance of this position, White's prospects still lie on the Kingside and Black's on the Queenside. Among top players former World Champion Boris Spassky has had many successes on the White side.

White has a number of choices for his 6th move, and formerly 6 B–K3, 6 KN–K2 and 6 N–R3 were all regularly played. Currently, however, 6 P–B4! is thought to be the most effective preparation for the intended Kingside play. Black should then choose a system which allows him to retain control of his strong point—the Q5 square—while also permitting a flexible response to White's Kingside play. Recommended, therefore, is 6 . . . P–K3! 7 N–B3 KN–K2! 8 0–0 0–0, since Black is always ready to counter White's P–KN4 with . . . P–KB4!.

Diffident play by Black can lead quickly to disaster. Instructive is Spassky–Geller, Match Game # 6, 1968: 6 . . . N–B3?! 7 N–B3 0–0 8 0–0 R–N1 9 P–KR3! P–QN4 10 P–R3! P–QR4 11 B–K3 P–N5 12 PxP RPxP 13 N–K2 B–N2 14 P–N3! R–R1 15 R–B1! R–R7 16 P–N4! Q–R1?! (Better was 16 . . . P–K3 or 16 . . . N–Q2) 17 Q–K1! Q–R3 18 Q–B2 N–R2?! (Better was 18 . . . N–Q2) 19 P–B5! N–N4 20 PxP RPxP 21 N–N5 N–R6 22 Q–R4! R–B1 23 RxN! PxR 24 Q–R7ch K–B1 25 NxP! RxP (After 25 . . . KxN decisive is 26 B–R6 R–KN1 27 N–B4!) 26 B–R6! RxRch 27 NxR KxN 28 QxBch K–K1 29 P–N5! P–B4 30 QxPch K–Q2 31 Q–B7ch K–B3 32 PxPch Black resigns.

2 . . . P–Q3

We shall use this flexible, popular and perfect move in our main line. This pawn move guards the key K4 square (thereby enabling . . . N–KB3 to be played, without having to worry about White's P–K5), opens the diagonal of the QB and entails no tactical or strategic deficiencies.

Of the possible alternatives, two are perfect and the others mediocre or inferior in various ways.

Downright poor is the immediate 2 . . . P–Q4? because after 3 PxP QxP 4 N–B3 Q–Q3 5 P–Q4 PxP White's superior development will lead to a lasting initiative after both 6 NxP and 6 QxP.

In the *mediocre* category are:

2 . . . P–QR3—The hope behind this move is that White will continue automatically with 3 P–Q4?!, whereupon Black, after 3 . . . PxP 4 NxP N–KB3 5 N–QB3 P–K4 6 N–N3 (or 6 N–B3) 6 . . . B–N5!, achieves smooth development of his Kingside and easy equality. Unfortunately, any reasonable third move by White, such as 3 P–B4 or 3 P–B3, stamps Black's 2 . . . P–QR3 as a loss of time and ensures White a steady edge.

2 . . . P–KN3—Aims for the immediate fianchetto of the KB.

Strategically the fianchetto is a perfectly sound idea (see our discussion of the Dragon Variation), but at the moment 3 P–Q4 is annoying, since 3 . . . PxP allows 4 QxP with an attack on the KR.

2 . . . N–KB3—This idea of Nimzovitch is analogous to the Alekhine Defense (1 P–K4 N–KB3), but is not as effective here since after 3 P–K5 it has been shown that the move . . . P–QB4 is less useful for Black than N–KB3 is for White.

Black's two *perfect* alternatives are:

(1) **2 . . . N–QB3**—Strategically the most logical follow-up to 1 . . . P–QB4: the QN is developed to its preferred central location from where it bears down on the key Q5 and K4 squares. There is "chessically" *nothing* wrong with the move; it does, however, preclude Black from playing certain currently popular variations such as the Najdorf and the Dragon. If Black continues with an early . . . P–Q3, then the same variations can occur as from 2 . . . P–Q3. The discussion of Black's 5th moves will make this clear.

The main independent lines that can occur after 2 . . . N–QB3 are: a) The Accelerated Dragon after 3 P–Q4 PxP 4 NxP P–KN3; b) The Taimanov after 3 P–Q4 PxP 4 NxP P–K3; c) The Sveshnikov–Lasker after 3 P–Q4 PxP 4 NxP N–KB3 5 N–QB3 P–K4. All of these are currently receiving extensive theoretical and practical testing.

(2) **2 . . . P–K3**—Black protects the key Q4 square and opens the diagonal for his KB. From the standpoint of opening principles the move must be rated perfect. If Black follows up with . . . P–Q3, then the same variations can occur as after 2 . . . P–Q3. If Black follows up with . . . N–QB3, then the same variations can occur as after 2 . . . N–QB3.

The most important independent line is the New Taimanov which results after 3 P–Q4 PxP 4 NxP P–QR3. It looks somewhat extravagant to me but is a popular guest in tournament play.

3 P–Q4

The most active and best move, successfully tested in thousands of master games. White opens both the QB's diagonal and the

DIAGRAM 19

BLACK

WHITE

Sicilian Defense
after 3 P–Q4

Q–file for the Queen, and, after the exchange of pawns in the center, will have the opportunity for active deployment of all the minor pieces. As Black's first move has done nothing for his Kingside development, rapid development of White's pieces will naturally give him good attacking chances against Black's King.

Grandmaster Bent Larsen of Denmark has made the perceptive remark that he does not really trust the accepted popular value of 3 P–Q4 because White voluntarily offers the strategically very valuable QP in exchange for the less valuable QBP. This analysis is true in so far as static strategic considerations apply. However, the specific dynamic situation must always be also considered. Here the dynamics cry out for an early opening of the position so that the inherent strength of 1 P–K4 can be utilized.

Instead of 3 P–Q4, White also has two other good moves:

(1) **3 N–B3**—The QN gets developed to its best square immediately. Black can't take advantage of the omission of 3 P–Q4 by playing 3 . . . P–K4?! since this allows White's KB to gain a very powerful diagonal after 4 B–B4. Black has therefore nothing better than 3 . . . N–KB3 or 3 . . . N–QB3,

and after 4 P–Q4 the game enters normal channels, albeit via transposition of moves.

(2) **3 B–N5ch**—Up until about 1970 this was thought to be a rather amateurish check, the continuation invariably being 3 . . . B–Q2 4 BxBch QxB 5 0–0. Even though White has castled rapidly, the exchange of Bishops has significantly decreased White's firepower, and Black equalizes rather easily. But the whole perspective on this check changed dramatically when the superficially logical 5 0–0 was replaced with the strategically motivated 5 P–B4!. This is one of the many, many variations which have been rehabilitated as a result of a deeper fundamental understanding of basic principles. The point of 5 P–B4 is to gain a very strong grip on the important Q5 square. Since the light–squared Bishops have been exchanged, White will not have to worry about his KB being locked in behind his own pawn formation. Thus, 5 P–B4 has no strategic deficiency. It also poses no tactical problems, since master practice has shown that the attempt to win a pawn with 5 . . . Q–N5? 6 0–0 QxKP leads to a decisive edge in development for White after 7 P–Q4!.

If Black develops routinely, then White will castle and play P–Q4. If Black tries to prevent P–Q4 by playing 5 . . . P–K4, then White will be left with the strategically superior Bishop, since Black's pawns will tend to hem in his KB. The overall evaluation of the position after 5 P–B4 is that White has a small, yet pleasant advantage entailing little risk. Therefore, Black has been trying out various other defenses, including 4 . . . NxB instead of 4 . . . QxB, as well as 3 . . . N–QB3 and 3 . . . N–Q2 in response to 3 B–N5ch. But in every case White can expect some initiative, and thus 3 B–N5ch is a fully viable alternative to 3 P–Q4.

3 . . . PxP

Black is not *forced* to capture, but why shouldn't he? As discussed earlier, he exchanges the QBP for White's valuable QP and opens his side of the QB–file for potential pressure by his QR and Queen against White's Queenside.

4 NxP

By far the most usual recapture. Yet here we have one of the rare instances where the apparently premature Queen development, 4 QxP, is also playable. This is so because the normal 4 . . . N–QB3 can be met by 5 B–QN5, and even though White will have to exchange off his KB, the resulting rapid development and retention of the Queen in the center of the board gives him fully satisfactory prospects. If Black prepares . . . N–QB3 with either 4 . . . P–QR3 or 4 . . . B–Q2, White plays 5 P–B4, and his increased central influence compensates for the tempo lost in retreating the Queen after 5 . . . N–QB3. Black, in theory, does have a shade easier task in equalizing against 4 QxP than against 4 NxP, yet in practice 4 QxP remains a perfectly reasonable alternative.

4 . . . N–KB3

Why not? The KN gets developed to its preferred square with a gain of time because the KP is attacked. The move is so perfect—not entailing even the smallest disadvantage—that there is *no* justification for playing anything else.

5 N–QB3

Developing the QN to its preferred square while doing the necessary job of protecting the KP is by far White's best move. Of course, the KP can be protected with 5 P–KB3, but why utilize a non–developmental move for this when a fine developmental one is available? At first glance the developmental 5 B–Q3 may also seem reasonable. Yet it suffers from a number of defects: (1) remembering the adage that "Knights should be developed before Bishops" again reminds us that it is still too early to know where the KB is placed best; (2) on Q3 the Bishop looks like an overgrown pawn and has no foreseeable offensive prospects; (3) by playing now 5 . . . N–B3 Black gains an important tempo for development, since White's Knight on Q4 is unprotected.

The position after White's 5 N–QB3 is the single most important basic position in the Sicilian Defense, because four very important variations begin at this point.

DIAGRAM 20

BLACK

WHITE

Sicilian Defense
after 5 N–QB3

Black here has four perfect moves. Three of these are easily derived from the basic principles of opening play. The fourth has been examined and proven sound in a colossal amount of analysis and practical play. These four perfect moves (variations) are:

(1) 5 . . . N–B3

From the viewpoints of development and center control, this is a perfect move. The QN gets developed to its preferred location without incurring the slightest inconvenience. The particular variation that results will be dependent on White's build–up. If he plays 6 B–K2, Black can transpose into Scheveningen lines via 6 . . . P–K3 or into the Dragon with 6 . . . P–KN3. The active 6 B–QB4—for many years the line Bobby Fischer played exclusively—brings about the Sozin Variation. Black's steadiest reply to this is 6 . . . P–K3, cramping White's KB.

White's most active and promising plan is the Richter–Rauser Attack with 6 B–KN5, which both prepares White for Queenside castling and makes it more difficult for Black to develop his Kingside smoothly. Thus 6 . . . P–KN3?! allows White to ruin Black's pawn formation with 7 BxN, while 6 . . . P–K3 voluntarily pins Black's KN. Still, the latter is Black's best move, and after White's 7 Q–Q2 Black has a fundamental choice to make. He can accept a solid, though somewhat passive, position after 7 . . . B–K2 8 0–0–0 0–0, or he can go in for immediate counterplay with 7 . . . P–QR3 8 0–0–0 B–Q2 9 P–B4 P–N4. The latter approach is currently more popular, though also unquestionably much more risky.

Note that the same position can be reached by the alternate move order 2 . . . N–QB3 3 P–Q4 PxP 4 NxP N–KB3 5 N–QB3 P–Q3.

(2) 5 . . . P–K3

The above move establishes the Scheveningen Variation, named after the Dutch town where the variation first gained popularity in tournament play. The Scheveningen is Black's most solid way of handling the inherently unbalanced Sicilian. The KP guards the important Q4 square and enables Black to play . . . B–K2, followed by Kingside castling. White, on his part, can also develop simply with 6 B–K2 and 7 0–0, a course favored by Karpov. Alternatively, White can try to take advantage of the fact that Black has voluntarily locked in both Bishops by playing the centrally sharp 6 P–B4 or the flanking super–sharp 6 P–KN4!?, the latter being the idea of grandmaster Paul Keres.

Note that the same position can be reached by the alternate move order 2 . . . P–K3 3 P–Q4 PxP 4 NxP N–KB3 5 N–QB3 P–Q3.

(3) 5 . . . P–KN3

Black will fianchetto the KB so that it bears down on the center and gets his King to safety by castling Kingside. This is the popular and important Dragon Variation. The Dragon makes strategic sense, is theoretically sound and leads to interesting tactics. It will be the variation considered in detail in Chapter Six, "Advanced Play."

(4) 5 . . . P–QR3

This is the world–famous Najdorf Variation. It is named after the Polish–Argentinian grandmaster Miguel (Misha)

Najdorf who popularized it after World War II. It was, however, Robert J. Fischer who made it famous as a result of his never–ending advocacy and successes. We know that it is sound, because of an immense amount of analytical work done by Fischer and his army of "Najdorf followers."

Let us look now at the move 5 . . . P–QR3 as it relates to the present situation on the chess board. It guards the QN4 square so that neither White's KB nor either of White's Knights can utilize it. Additionally, Black prepares to play a timely . . . P–QN4. This is all that it does. Are these of substantial importance? No, they are not. Does Black do anything to further his development, central control or prospects of castling? No, he doesn't. What Black is doing is to throw a psychological challenge to White to "come and get him." Black is playing the already risky Sicilian almost a whole tempo down (5 . . . P–QR3 is a *shade* better than making no move at all). As I said earlier, the Najdorf is sound theoretically. Sound that is for a Fischer, or someone equally well versed in reams of recent analysis. It is extremely difficult for anyone else to play because the variations are based not so much on strategic principles as on specific, sharp, complicated "blow by blow" calculations. The average player employing the Najdorf assumes a considerably greater than average risk, with less than an average hope of success. Remember that Black is playing almost a whole move behind!

What can White do against the Najdorf? Obviously, many things. At one extreme, he can ignore it and develop with 6 B–K2 followed by Kingside castling. Anatoly Karpov plays in this way, saying that "there is absolutely no reason to give Black any of the hoped–for counterchances." At the other extreme, White can immediately go after Black's King with 6 B–KN5 P–K3 7 P–B4. Variations emanating from 6 B–KN5 are extremely complicated, tactical, long, difficult—and continually changing. Middle ground possibilities include such continuations as 6 P–QR4 and 6 P–B4.

Except for the "perfect four" discussed above, all other Black moves are inferior. I will make special mention only of 5 . . . P–K4?! because that is a favorite among many amateurs.

DIAGRAM 21

BLACK

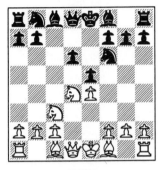

WHITE

Sicilian Defense
after 5 . . . P-K4?!

This move finds favor because, I guess, it looks good to some: White's KN is driven from its central location, and the pawn on K4 is centrally more active than, say, on K2. However, the disadvantages it entails are severe. First of all, Black *permanently* weakens his important Q4 square, since he no longer has a pawn available to protect it. Secondly, the QP on Q3 will be backward and vulnerable to an attack on the Queen-file. Moreover, Black's KB is sentenced to a life of dreary passivity. On K2 it has no scope and functions mostly to protect the QP. If it is fianchettoed (placed on KN2), it also has few prospects, since the Black pawn on K4 severely limits its scope. Additionally, with the Bishop on KN2, the QP may be very weak.

White's most effective response is immediately to take advantage of the weakening of the light squares in Black's position by playing 6 B-N5ch. After 6 . . . QN-Q2 White has 7 N-B5, and after 6 . . . B-Q2 White plays 7 BxBch QxB   8 N-B3.

CHAPTER 6
Sicilian Defense: Advanced Play

The majority of the variations in the Sicilian Defense do follow the logical requirements of good opening principles. A deeper and longer look at one of them can illustrate very well the general theme of "how to play good opening moves." Moreover, such an investigation will also teach much about the strategies and tactics involved in the Sicilian. For this closer look into the Sicilian, I have selected the Dragon Variation. As already mentioned in Chapter 5, the Dragon both makes a lot of strategic sense and leads to thematic, sharp tactics.

Our starting point is the position after 1 P–K4 P–QB4   2 N–KB3 P–Q3   3 P–Q4 PxP   4 NxP N–KB3   5 N–QB3 P–KN3.

The most important characteristics of the Dragon from the points of view of both White and Black are:

1. The obvious follow-up to 5 . . . P–KN3 is to fianchetto the KB by . . . B–KN2 so that it exerts pressure along the center diagonal. Since Black is ready for Kingside castling as soon as . . . B–KN2 has been played, the Kingside is the logical place for Black's King.

2. The central pawn formation is in White's favor, since his KP on K4 controls more space than Black's QP on Q3. As is generally true in the Sicilian, if Black can play . . . P–Q4 without disadvantage, he will have sound equality.

3. The move 5 . . . P–KN3 has led to a slight but fundamental weakening of Black's Kingside, since Black's KNP can now be attacked by a White KRP on R5. This in turn will lead to the opening of a file on the Kingside, most likely the KR–file.

DIAGRAM 22

BLACK

WHITE

Sicilian Defense
Dragon Variation
after 5 . . . P–KN3

4. White has the option of castling on either side. Of course, castling Kingside is inherently safer. However, the Queenside is reasonably safe on a short–term basis, and castling there allows White the prospects of an attack against Black's Kingside. The key elements in this attack are the opening of the KR–file and the exchanging off of Black's KB via B–KR6.

Let us now look at the Dragon Variation's main lines and significant alternatives. From the starting point of Diagram 22, the play develops as follows:

6 B–K3

With both Knights developed, White's next goal is to bring out the Bishops. The QB seemingly has two logical posts: KN5 and K3. Though 6 B–KN5 looks good at first glance, the attack on the KN is blunted by the simple 6 . . . B–N2. Moreover, Black will get counterchances against White's loosely protected Q4 square (i.e., the KN). On the other hand, 6 B–K3 develops the QB to a flexible, centrally supportive square with no drawbacks. The move even contains a sneaky trap. If Black gets too frisky and plays 6 . . . N–N5?, White's 7 B–N5ch! leads to heavy gain of material after 7 . . . B–Q2 8 QxN.

White could also develop his KB first, placing it either on QB4 or K2. However, since the best square of the QB is already known, it is somewhat more flexible to develop it first. Play usually different from the main line of the Dragon ensues if White plays 6 P–B4, the Löwenfish Variation. Black's soundest counter is 6 . . . N–B3, when the position after 7 NxN PxN   8 P–K5 N–Q2!   9 PxP PxP offers approximately equal chances. The strategic fault of the Löwenfish is that, as can be easily seen, White's central superiority has disappeared, while Black's position remains sufficiently sound.

6 . . . B–N2

Since this is the idea behind 5 . . . P–KN3, there is absolutely no reason not to play it immediately. From a practical standpoint, however, 6 . . . N–B3 is equivalent.

7 P–B3

The introduction to the Yugoslav Attack, whereby White will continue with Q–Q2 and castle Queenside. The preparatory text serves a number of functions: Black's annoying . . . N–KN5 is prevented, the KP securely protected and the potential Kingside advance P–KN4 prepared. The Yugoslav Attack is by far the sharpest way for White to fight the Dragon and is the most popular method in master praxis.

Fully sound, however, is the so-called "old" or "normal" variation, whereby White castles Kingside. The key position in this line arises after 7 B–K2 N–B3   8 0–0 0–0. White cannot immediately attack on the Kingside with 9 P–B4?! since Black then plays 9 . . . Q–N3! with a simple attack on the QNP and a camouflaged attack on the KN (the threat being 10 . . . NxP!, winning the KP). Black, for his part, being castled, is ready to play 9 . . . P–Q4, a move that equalizes after 9 P–B3, 9 P–KR3 or 9 K–R1 and leads to just a tiny disadvantage after 9 Q–Q2.

Main line play results after 9 N–N3 B–K3   10 P–B4, with Black having two methods to cope with White's planned P–KB5. In the older Maroczy Variation Black plays 10 . . . N–QR4, in order to continue with 11 . . . B–B5 after 11 P–B5. In the newer Tartakower Variation Black prevents P–KB5 by 10 . . . Q–B1 and then aims to get in . . . P–Q4 by playing R–Q1. In either case, Black can expect approximate equality in due course.

7 . . . N–B3

Developing the QN to its best square is a perfect move.

8 Q–Q2

Continuing with the plan of getting ready for Queenside castling.

8 . . . 0–0

Even though it can be clearly anticipated that White will try to attack on the Kingside, Black's King will still be safer there than in the center. Moreover, the KR is brought into play and his chances for . . . P–Q4 increased. Castling Queenside is not viable, since not only is the King exposed there (the QBP is missing!), but also Black's thematic attacking chances lie along the QB file, and the presence of his King in this sector will hamper his counterplay significantly.

9 B–QB4

The newer and most common move. The Bishop is aggressively posted to attack the KB7 square and Black's freeing . . . P–Q4 inhibited. However, there also is an unavoidable drawback involved: the Bishop's unprotected status on QB4 will allow Black to gain a tempo or two for his own development.

Also playable and good is the older 9 0–0–0. Black then has the double-edged option of 9 . . . P–Q4!?, leading to 10 PxP NxP 11 NxN/6 PxN. Analysis and practical play have shown that Black does not have to worry about losing a pawn after 12 NxN PxN 13 QxP, since with 13 . . . Q–B2! he gets excellent attacking chances along the half-open QN and QB files (14 QxR?! B–B4! leads to advantage for Black). Current master thinking is that White should play strategically with 12 B–Q4! P–K4 13 B–B5 B–K3! 14 N–K4!, leading to a slightly more pleasant position for White, since after 14 . . . R–K1 15 P–KR4! White still has attacking chances on the Kingside, whereas Black's KB is dormant and the pin along the Q–file can prove to be annoying.

9 . . . B–Q2!

On the face of it quite logical: the last minor piece is developed and the way freed for . . . R–QB1 to start counterplay along the

QB–file. Still it took the master fraternity a long time—over six years—to discover it! The explanation is that they were so terrorized by the apparent power of White's KB that it was felt *immediate* steps must be taken to neutralize its power. Thus the Blacks tried 9 . . . NxN 10 BxN B–K3, 9 . . . N–QR4, 9 . . . N–Q2 followed by 10 . . . N–N3 and 11 . . . N–R4, 9 . . . P–QR3, 9 . . . P–QR4—and all for naught. Since nothing exotic worked, the decision was made to go back to basics and, lo and behold, Black began to secure good chances. This is one of the best examples of how correct application of basic opening principles—completion of development prior to starting action, importance of central influence, etc.—could have saved many masters much grief.

DIAGRAM 23

BLACK

WHITE

Sicilian Defense
Dragon Variation
after 9 . . . B–Q2!

10 P–KR4

The two inherent aspects of White's future strategy are attack along the KR–file and castling Queenside. It probably does not matter too much whether White first plays 10 0–0–0 or 10 P–KR4. Currently, however, master practice prefers the sharper text move, since it entails no disadvantages and immediately subjects Black to a sharp attack.

Even though White's KB is vulnerable on QB4, that is *no* reason *voluntarily* to lose a tempo by retreating it to QN3. After 10 B–N3?! Black can immediately start a promising Queenside action with 10 . . . NxN! 11 BxN P–QN4!, to be followed by . . . P–QR4. This leads to fully equal counterchances for Black, since White's KB occupies a precarious position. Remember: Do not waste time with unnecessary retreats when the position requires sharp play by both sides!

The text move tells Black without a shadow of doubt what is coming: a sharp, direct attack on his King. How should he respond? Two general approaches are feasible: (1) immediately to counterattack on the Queenside, or (2) to try to combine counterattack with defense.

10 . . . P–KR4

Master practice in the early 1980's has given preference to the approach in which Black tries to slow down White's attack along the KR–file. The text move does exactly that, but at a very clear and obvious cost: a fundamental weakening of Black's Kingside pawn formation. Moreover, Black will be a move behind in his efforts at counterplay.

The alternative plan is to start an immediate counterattack. Since sharp, tactical sub-variations can easily gain or lose popularity, the "immediate counter-attack" variations may reappear in master practice at any time. Such a variation is well demonstrated in the course of A. Karpov–V. Korchnoi, Match Game # 2, 1974:

10 . . . R–B1 (Threatening to win material with 11 . . . NxN.) 11 B–N3 N–K4 (Immediately going for counterplay along the QB file.) 12 0–0–0 N–B5 13 BxN (The necessity for this capture shows up the major strategic disadvantage of 9 B–QB4: White's KB has made two moves just to be exchanged off for Black's QN on a square which the Bishop controls equally well from KB1!) 13 . . . RxB 14 P–R5! (As compared to the preparatory 14 P–KN4, White saves 1 or 2 moves for the opening of the KR–file by sacrificing the KRP.) 14 . . . NxRP 15 P–KN4 N–B3 16 N/4–K2!

(A multipurpose move: (1) The QB3 Knight is overprotected, thus making it difficult for Black to gain counterchances with

DIAGRAM 24

BLACK

WHITE

Karpov–Korchnoi
1974 Match
after 16 N/4–K2!

the characteristic . . . RxN/6 sacrifice, (2) the Knight can move to KN3 or KB4 for attacking purposes, (3) B–R6 is threatened. The immediate 16 B–R6?! allows 16 . . . NxKP! 17 Q–K3 RxN/6!, with Black having sufficient counterplay.) 16 . . . Q–R4 (Counterattack!) 17 B–R6 (Exchanging off Black's valuable offensive and defensive Bishop.) 17 . . . BxB 18 QxB KR–B1 (Counterattack!) 19 R–Q3! (Again preventing the counterplay resulting from an exchange sacrifice on White's QB3. Black should now neutralize White's attack with 19 . . . Q–Q1 20 P–N5 N–R4 21 N–N3 Q–B1, after which White will regain the pawn and keep a slight endgame edge.) 19 . . . R/5–B4? 20 P–N5!! RxP (Forced.) 21 R–Q5!! (White's 20th and 21st moves together comprise a brilliant concept to attack Black's weak point: the KRP. Black is lost.) 21 . . . RxR 22 NxR R–K1 23 N/2–B4! B–B3 24 P–K5!! BxN (White's powerful 24th move prevents a Black Queen check on KN4 in the following variation: 24 . . . PxP 25 NxNch PxN 26 N–R5! PxN 27 R–N1ch.) 25 PxN PxP 26 QxRPch K–B1 27 Q–R8ch and Black resigns, since after 27 . . . K–K2 28 NxBch QxN 29 R–K1ch he loses heavy material.

11 0-0-0

With his immediate attacking prospects stopped, it is quite in order for White to complete Queenside development by castling.

11 . . . R–B1   12 B–N3

The threat of 12 . . . NxN forces the Bishop to retreat.

12 . . . N–K4

The critical position in this sub-variation. Black is ready to inaugurate his play along the QB file with 13 . . . N–B5, whereas White's attack seems stymied. The following choices for White must be considered:

(1) *Brute force*—White plays 13 P–KN4?!: Black's position is sufficiently sound, and after 13 . . . PxP   14 P–R5 NxRP 15 B–R6 P–K3! he has every reason to expect that he will weather White's attack successfully.

(2) *Quiet preparation*—White plays 13 K–N1: Black achieves approximate equality after the thematic 13 . . . N–B5   14 BxN RxB   15 N–N3 Q–B2.

(3) *Strategic exchange*—White plays 13 B–R6: Though the exchange of the dark square Bishops is of strategic value to White, Black has the following tactical method of gaining full counterplay: 13 . . . BxB!   14 QxB RxN!   15 PxR Q–R4 16 K–N2 R–B1. White's weakened King position and pawn structure give Black full compensation for the exchange.

Since White must do something, even though no truly forceful action is available, the best move is:

13 B–N5!

A creative change of plan. White cannot achieve anything immediately against Black's Kingside, although Black's weaknesses there do give White *long-term* prospects. White therefore prepares for action in the center. Black cannot chase the annoying Bishop away with 13 . . . N–R2?!, since the misplacement of the Knight means that after 14 B–R6! BxB   15 QxB, the exchange sacrifice 15 . . . RxN does not yield full compensation anymore.

13 . . . R–B4!

Black gets ready to start counterplay with 14 . . . P–N4, while giving additional support to his central squares, particularly K4. The latent power of White's 13 B–N5 makes it impossible for Black to execute more conventional plans under satisfactory conditions. Thus 13 . . . Q–R4?! is met by 14 K–N1!, and already White threatens 15 BxN! BxB 16 N–Q5, ruining Black's pawn formation. If 13 . . . N–B5?!, then 14 KBxN! RxB 15 N–N3!, and White threatens the annoying 16 P–K5! since 16 . . . PxP leads to the loss of a piece after 17 BxN!.

From here on, we shall follow the game A. Karpov–G. Sosonko, Tilburg 1979:

DIAGRAM 25

BLACK

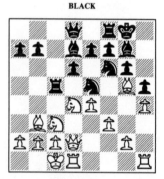

WHITE

Karpov–Sosonko
Tilburg 1979
after 13 . . . R–B4!

14 KR–K1 !?

Since White's immediate prospects lie in the central break P–K5, he puts maximum power behind it. Less effective is the immediate 14 P–B4, since after 14 . . . N–B5 15 Q–Q3 P–N4 16 P–K5, Black gets excellent counterplay with 16 . . . Q–N3!. Note that White cannot win a piece with 17 PxN since after 17 . . . PxP his QB is trapped.

14 . . . P–N4

Black starts his counterattack.

15 P–B4

Everything is set for the coming P–K5 break and there is no time to tarry.

15 . . . N–B5   16 KBxN PxB?

Black hopes to gain counterplay along the QN file, but there will not be sufficient time for it. Therefore, correct and necessary is 16 . . . RxKB. Then, after 17 P–K5, Black can counter with 17 . . . P–N5   18 PxN PxP!. Other 17th moves for White should also allow Black sufficient counterplay. Of course, the specific possibilities can turn out to be exceedingly complicated—as is characteristic of the Yugoslav Attack against the Dragon.

17 BxN!!

Played with great insight into the position. As the note to White's 14th move shows, the QB is vulnerable on KN5, and White therefore exchanges it off. After the routine 17 P–K5?! Black would indeed get a very strong attack with 17 . . . Q–N3!   18 PxN R–N1. After the text, 17 . . . PxB would lock in the KB and leave the QP vulnerable, allowing White to gain a big edge with either 18 N–B3 or 18 P–B5.

17 . . . BxB   18 P–K5! B–N2

There is no choice, since both 18 . . . PxP?   19 N–B3!, and 18 . . . BxRP?   19 R–R1 are totally unsatisfactory for Black.

19 P–K6!

Notice how the central advance is ultimately used for the further weakening of Black's Kingside.

19 . . . B–B1   20 PxPch RxP   21 N–K6 QBxN   22 RxB Q–R4!?

Aiming for the most counterplays possible under the circumstances. If White rushes things with 23 RxNP?!, then after 23 . . . K–R2! Black would stand reasonably, since 24 R–N5 BxN forces 25 QxB with an equal endgame.

23 Q–K3!

Increasing the pressure on Black's position *and* giving White's King a flight square on Q2.

23 . . . BxN

The resulting Queenside attacking chances are not sufficient to compensate for the mortal weakening of the King position. However, even after the slightly better 23 . . . B–B3, White, with 24 N–K4!, sets unsolvable problems for Black.

24 PxB QxRP 25 RxPch K–B1 26 Q–K4!

The centralized Queen threatens 27 Q–R8ch and is also ready to shift to the Kingside if necessary.

26 . . . Q–R3 27 R–Q5!

Exchanging off one Rook allows White to break into Black's position with decisive effect. The elegant refutation to 27 . . . Q–B3 is 28 RxR!.

27 . . . R–KB3 28 RxR/5 RxR 29 RxRP P–Q4 30 RxP Black resigns

He is two pawns down and remains in danger of being mated.

CHAPTER 7
Queen's Gambit Declined: Basic Principles

During most of the 19th century, Romanticism and attack was the order of the day, and White's first move was invariably 1 P–K4. However, near the end of the century the top players realized that opening the game with 1 P–Q4 also had much chess logic behind it. In one area there was no disagreement at all: the only correct reply to 1 P–Q4 was thought to be 1 . . . P–Q4. The reasoning behind 1 . . . P–Q4 was (and still is) fully sound. Black imitates White's strong central move and will fight to retain control of his important Q4 square. Since the Queen already protects this square from its original position, Black's task in protecting Q4 is considerably easier than in protecting K4 in the openings starting with 1 P–K4 P–K4. Because of its inherent soundness, the Queen's Gambit Declined has stood the test of time, and in the 1980's has the same good reputation as it enjoyed one hundred years earlier.

The most important characteristic of 1 . . . P–Q4, followed by 2 . . . P–K3, is its solidity. It is preferred by masters who are quite willing to defend a slightly cramped position in order to achieve safe and sound equality in due course. White's play in the Queen's Gambit generally starts off on the Queen's side of the center. However, opening the center can easily swing the scene of action to the Kingside. Black's approach in general is to defend whatever area White is attacking. Black's opportunities for counterplay will usually arise whenever White has overextended himself somewhere.

Of course, specific variations have their own particular points. The main line and significant alternatives are as follows:

1 P–Q4 P–Q4   2 P–QB4

DIAGRAM 26

BLACK

WHITE

1 P–Q4 P–Q4
2 P–QB4
The Queen's Gambit

White immediately attacks Black's key central outpost, the QP, from the flank. This opening is called the Queen's Gambit. The name is something of a misnomer, however. The word "gambit" suggests sacrifice or risk, and in the Queen's Gambit White sacrifices and risks nothing. Black can capture the QBP, but he cannot afford to hold on to it. For instance, after 2 . . . PxP   3 N–KB3 P–QR3   4 P–K3 P–QN4?!   5 P–QR4 White is sure to recover his pawn with a greater-than-normal advantage. Two examples: 5 . . . P–QB3   6 PxP BPxP   7 P–QN3! PxP   8 BxPch!, or 5 . . . B–N2   6 P–QN3!.

Nevertheless, 2 . . . PxP plays an accepted role in opening theory and is called the Queen's Gambit Accepted. After 3 N–KB3 Black gives back the captured pawn and tries to complete his development quickly. The two main approaches are: (1) 3 . . . P–QR3   4 P–K3 B–N5   5 BxP P–K3   6 P–KR3 B–R4 7 N–B3 N–KB3   8 0–0 N–B3   9 B–K2 B–Q3, and (2) 3 . . .

N–KB3 4 P–K3 P–K3 5 BxP P–B4 6 0–0 P–QR3 7 Q–K2
P–QN4 8 B–N3 B–N2. As can be seen, in each case Black's basic
development is sound, yet White has a noticeable central
superiority. According to official opening theory, the Queen's
Gambit Accepted is a fully satisfactory opening system. Still,
White's central superiority, attained with little risk, suggests to
me that the White side is considerably easier to handle than the
Black side. The popularity of the QGA has fluctuated
throughout the years. In the 1980's it is on the upswing again.

2 . . . P–K3

The primary goal of 1 . . . P–Q4 is to control the important
Q4 and K5 central squares. Black's second move should be
consistent with this plan. Therefore completely wrong—though
common in amateur chess—is 2 . . . N–KB3?, since after 3 PxP
Black's thematic central influence has largely disappeared and
White will soon attain a substantial central and strategic
superiority.

To fortify Q4 Black must play either 2 . . . P–K3 or 2 . . .
P–QB3. The more common move is 2 . . . P–K3, bringing about
variations of the so-called Orthodox Defense of the Queen's
Gambit Declined. The move has the obvious advantage of
furthering Kingside development and castling. There is one
strategic disadvantage, however; the QB is locked in behind its
KP.

The logic behind 2 . . . P–QB3—the Slav Defense—is that Q4
is supported while the diagonal of the QB remains open. Yet
there is a small problem with the Slav also: after 3 N–QB3 N–B3
4 N–B3 how is Black to develop his KB? If now 4 . . . P–K3,
the QB is again locked in, whereas 4 . . . P–KN3 leads to a
passive variation of the Gruenfeld Defense (1 P–Q4 N–KB3 2
P–QB4 P–KN3 3 N–QB3 P–Q4). The development of the QB
with 4 . . . B–B4, although it may appear logical, unfortunately
leads to difficulties with the protection of the Queenside after 5
PxP! PxP 6 Q–N3!. Thus Black has nothing better than to give
up the center by 4 . . . PxP.

The redeeming factor for Black in this is that White cannot
smoothly recover his pawn with the desirable 5 P–K3 or 5 P–K4
because, under the changed circumstances, Black can play 5 . . .

P–QN4 with good effect. Therefore, White must prevent that move by first playing 5 P–QR4, yet that move has two drawbacks: one tempo is lost and the QN4 square permanently weakened. These factors allow Black to achieve a satisfactory position as follows: 5 . . . B–B4 (to control K5.) 6 P–K3 P–K3 (to develop the Kingside.) 7 BxP B–QN5 (to develop the Kingside and control K5 indirectly.) 8 0–0 0–0 9 Q–K2 QN–Q2 (Completing the development of the minor pieces.)

DIAGRAM 27

BLACK

WHITE

Slav Defense
after 9 . . . QN–Q2

This is a key position in the Slav Defense. White has a central advantage and can enhance it after 10 P–K4 B–N3. Yet Black's position is very solid and his minor pieces well developed. Thus Black's ultimate disadvantage is just a small one.

3 N–QB3

From the standpoint of strategic principles the most logical follow-up. The QN is immediately developed to its ideal square, from where it attacks Q5 and protects K4. From a practical standpoint 3 N–KB3 is about equivalent. However, 3 N–QB3 is thought to be a shade more accurate, since Black's QP is under pressure and White retains more flexibility in the immediate future. That is, N–QB3 is important to all of White's possible plans, whereas the development of the KN may be delayed in certain variations.

3 . . . N–KB3

In every respect a perfect move: the KN is developed to its ideal square, protecting Q4 and enabling Black to castle rapidly.

There are two other possibilities that occur often in master chess. The first is 3 . . . B–K2, a sophisticated way of preventing White's immediate B–KN5, which, however, only is of significance if White intends to play the Exchange Variation (PxP on the 3rd, 4th or 5th move). I'll have more to say about this a bit later on.

Black's second alternative is a major one: 3 . . . P–QB4, leading to the Tarrasch Defense to the QGD. In exchange for an isolated QP, Black obtains free piece play and good central presence. The popularity of the Tarrasch has had many ups and downs, and in the 1980's is on the upswing again. Among the recent world champions, Boris Spassky sometimes plays it. The main line variation occurs after 4 QPxP KPxP   5 N–B3 N–QB3   6 P–KN3! N–B3   7 B–N2 B–K2   8 0–0 0–0.

DIAGRAM 28

BLACK

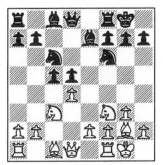

WHITE

Tarrasch Defense
after 8 . . . O–O

White has developed his KB so that it is trained on Black's isolated QP. The normal moves for White now are 9 PxP and 9

B–N5, and with either one he can expect a slight advantage. On the other hand, Black's development is sound and his prospects no worse than in other defenses to the Queen's Gambit.

4 N–B3

Developing the KN to its ideal square furthers all three opening objectives. Equally good is 4 B–N5, which after 4 . . . B–K2   5 N–B3 leads to our main line.

White can also choose a radically different plan, the so-called Exchange Variation: 4 PxP PxP   5 B–N5 B–K2   6 P–K3 0–0 (6 . . . B–KB4? fails to 7 Q–N3!) 7 B–Q3. Though the central tension has been resolved, White retains a number of small advantages: (1) the exchange of the QBP for the KP gives White greater central influence, (2) White's light square Bishop is more active than its counterpart, (3) White has attacking chances against Black's Queenside along the QB file (if Black plays . . . P–QB3, White will attack this with P–QN4, followed by P–QN5—this is called a "minority attack"). In general, this move order in the Exchange Variation gives White a comfortable opening advantage. However, the play takes on "drier" characteristics than in the main line and thus is not up everyone's alley.

4 . . . B–K2

The standard move. Black anticipates White's B–N5 and gets ready for castling. Three other, significantly different, plans are also possible. With 4 . . . B–N5 Black enters the Ragozin Variation, a cross between the Queen's Gambit Declined and the Nimzo–Indian Defense (1 P–Q4 N–KB3   2 P–QB4 P–K3   3 N–QB3 B–N5). Early in his career, this was a favorite of Fischer's, although he achieved only mediocre results with it. Usually mixing two systems achieves nothing but indigestion, and here, too, after 5 B–N5 P–KR3   6 BxN QxB   7 P–K3 0–0   8 R–B1 White has somewhat more prospect for a sustained advantage than in the main lines, mainly because Black's KB on QN5 isn't doing very much.

Black's other two choices involve moving the QBP. After 4 . . . P–B4   5 BPxP NxP (5 . . . KPxP transposes into the Tarrasch) the Semi-Tarrasch Variation is reached. Unlike in the Tarrasch, Black does not have to worry about an isolated QP, but, on the other hand, has less central influence. White can exploit this factor either by the sharp 6 P–K4 or the modest 6 P–K3, and, in each case, retain slightly superior chances.

Considerably trickier than it appears is the passive looking 4 . . . P–B3. Its tactical point is that after the "normal" 5 B–N5, Black can capture and hold on to the QBP. This is called the Botvinnik Variation and leads to tremendous complications after 5 . . . PxP 6 P–K4 P–N4! 7 P–K5 P–KR3 8 B–R4 P–N4. Chess theory has not yet given a definitive answer regarding the value of the sub-variations that occur. Moreover, when White plays the strategic 1 P–Q4, he is looking forward to a quieter life than is possible in the Botvinnik variation. Therefore, White usually responds with the modest 5 P–K3, voluntarily locking in his QB. This brings about the Meran Variation, with the main line going: 5 . . . QN–Q2 6 B–Q3 PxP 7 BxBP P–QN4 8 B–Q3. Now Black plays either 8 . . . P–QR3 or 8 . . . B–N2, in each case aiming for an early . . . P–QB4. Of course, White retains some central pull after 9 P–K4, and with it the usual slight advantage.

5 B–N5

The QB is developed to an active square and the attack against the Knight means an indirect increase in the pressure on Q5. Not as common, but also perfectly playable, is 5 B–B4. However, premature is the immediate attempt at furthering Kingside development with 5 P–K3?!, since that would unnecessarily lock in the QB.

Note also that the attempt to enter the Exchange Variation now brings no advantage. After 5 PxP PxP 6 B–N5 P–B3! 7 P–K3 (or 7 Q–B2 P–KN3! followed by 8 . . . B–KB4) 7 . . . B–KB4 Black's QB is well developed, and this is sufficient to equalize prospects.

5 . . . 0–0!

Yes! Rapid castling is an important opening goal and is of greater necessity for Black than for White. There is absolutely no reason not to complete Kingside development by castling. Pointless is the passive 5 . . . P–B3, since Black's QP is already sufficiently protected, and at some future time Black may want to challenge White's QP via . . . P–QB4. It is obviously time–saving to execute that move in one step rather than two.

6 P–K3

With White's QB now developed, it is in order to work on completing the development of the Kingside. At this point the text move entails no disadvantages.

6 . . . P–KR3

The most popular move of the 1970's and 1980's. Black slightly weakens his King position, but the closed nature of the position and White's expected castling on the Kingside means that the opponent will not be able to take advantage of this slight weakening. Black also has no need to fear 7 BxN BxB, since he can readily protect Q4.

From a positive standpoint, 6 . . . P–KR3 has two virtues: (1) the KRP is not vulnerable to an anticipated attack by White's Q–B2 and B–Q3, and (2) White's QB is made to declare its intentions.

The time–tested alternative is the "classical" 6 . . . QN–Q2. This inaugurates a sound though passive plan, whereby Black will slowly aim for an eventual equality. The main line is 7 R–B1 P–B3 8 B–Q3 PxP   9 BxBP N–Q4; in this particular approach it is easier for Black to force piece exchanges if White's QB is on KN5, and therefore in this instance having played the move . . . P–KR3 would not be advantageous.

7 B–R4

It is consistent to retain the "semi–pin" secured by 5 B–N5.

This position is the starting point for a number of possible variations in the Orthodox Defense to the Queen's Gambit Declined. A comparison of the development of each side leads to the following evaluation: White, as a result of having his QBP on QB4, has more central influence, and his three developed minor pieces work on important central squares. White's Kingside development has lagged, but the still–closed nature of the position means that his King is in no immediate danger. Black, for his part, has completed his Kingside development and brought his King to safety by castling. Moreover, his central bastion on Q4 is quite secure.

DIAGRAM 29

BLACK

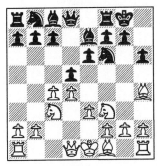

WHITE

Queen's Gambit Declined
after 7 B–R4

White's short–term plan is clear: he wants to complete his Kingside development. But what should Black aim for now? Actually, Black has three reasonable approaches:

1. Lasker's Freeing Maneuver: **7 . . . N–K5.**

Black's position is somewhat cramped, of course, and the standard technique for freeing cramped positions is to exchange pieces. The text accomplishes this after the usual moves 8 BxB QxB 9 PxP NxN 10 PxN PxP. However, these exchanges have led to a strengthening of White's center, since his QNP has been transformed into a QBP. This factor allows White to obtain a slight advantage as follows: 11 Q–N3! R–Q1 12 P–B4! PxP 13 BxP N–B3 14 B–K2. Whether Black exchanges Queens or not, White will castle Kingside, and his central superiority will offer him somewhat better chances.

2. The delayed classical **7 . . . QN–Q2.**

Now after 8 R–B1 P–B3 9 B–Q3 PxP 10 BxP, 10 . . . N–Q4?! is not efficient, since after 11 B–KN3! Black has nothing to show for his decreased central influence. However, the sharper 10 . . . P–QN4!? 11 B–Q3 P–R3, whereby Black aims to challenge White's center with . . . P–QB4 (e.g., 12 0–0 P–B4), gives Black prospects for eventual equality.

3. Tartakower's **7 . . . P–QN3.**

This will be our main line and will be discussed in detail in Chapter 8.

Other moves by Black are either inadvisable or downright poor. Thus 7 . . . N–R4? blunders away a pawn after 8 BxB QxB 9 PxP, whereas 7 . . . P–B4?! leads to an isolated and vulnerable QP after 8 BPxP KPxP 9 PxP.

CHAPTER 8
Queen's Gambit Declined: Advanced Play

Our starting point is the position after White's 7th move: 1 P–Q4 P–Q4 2 P–QB4 P–K3 3 N–QB3 N–KB3 4 N–B3 B–K2 5 B–N5 0–0 6 P–K3 P–KR3 7 B–R4. What is and what is not in order in Black's position? Well, he has brought his King to safety by castling, his Kingside is well developed and has no noticeable weaknesses, his central influence is good. Black's only real strategic problem is the lack of scope for his QB. Black's KP hems in the QB, and, unless White voluntarily plays PxP, thus enabling Black to recapture with his KP, the QB will remain locked in for a long time to come. During the London tournament of 1922, the Polish–French grandmaster Savielly Tartakower hit on the idea of trying to do something about the "QB problem" immediately by fianchettoing it. In his game against Capablanca he played:

7 . . . P–QN3

Black's idea is disarmingly simple and completely sound: he will follow up with the centrally logical 8 . . . B–N2 and the supposedly permanent problem of the QB will have been solved in an instant! Since its introduction, the Tartakower Variation has been Black's most popular way of defending the Orthodox QGD. Among recent world champions who have employed it successfully are Boris Spassky, Robert J. Fischer and Anatoly Karpov. The special practical value of the Tartakower Variation

DIAGRAM 30

BLACK

WHITE

Queen's Gambit Declined
after 7 . . . P–QN3

is that it combines strategic soundness with an unbalanced position. This means that not only does Black have excellent prospects for equality, but, if White does not play correctly, he can very easily get the worst of the position.

If White does nothing—that is, ignores Black's plan—his chances for an opening advantage are non-existent. This was well demonstrated in V. Korchnoi–A. Karpov, 1978 World Championship Match, Game # 1: 8 R–B1 B–N2 9 B–Q3 PxP 10 BxP QN–Q2 11 0–0 P–B4 12 PxP NxP 13 Q–K2 P–R3! 14 KR–Q1 Q–K1! 15 P–QR3 N/3–K5! 16 NxN NxN 17 BxB QxB 18 N–Q4 KR–B1!. Draw agreed. The pawn formation is almost symmetrical and the position and chances fully equal.

Therefore, to hope for an advantage, White must try to cross up Black's plan. But how?

8 PxP

The only strategic drawback of 7 . . . P–QN3 is the slight yet permanent weakening of Black's QB3 square. The idea behind the text move is to try to take advantage of this by quickly organizing pressure along the QB–file against Black's Queenside.

There is another sophisticated approach for exploiting the weakness of Black's QB3. It stems from Viktor Korchnoi and consists of the plan 8 BxN!? BxB 9 PxP PxP. It appears that White could have saved a whole tempo by playing the immediate 7 BxN, but this loss of time is more than counterbalanced by the creation of the weakness at Black's QB3. Though Black is allowed the two Bishops, this is of no advantage here because the soundness of White's pawn chain means that there is nothing vulnerable in White's position for the Bishops to attack. On the other hand, White's nimble Knights can be maneuvered to attack Black's QP. This will force Black to play . . . P–QB3, leading to a weakened QBP. White will then try to work directly against this on the QB–file or will open the center advantageously via P–K4. Since the advent of Korchnoi's idea, there have been further small improvements in the execution of White's plan. White often plays 8 B–K2 or 8 Q–N3 first, in order to induce Black to play 8 . . . B–N2. This way, Black's Bishop is denied a potentially more useful location on K3.

For an overall appreciation of White's strategy, A. Karpov–B. Spassky, 1974 World Championship Semi-Final Candidates Match, Game # 11, is a good example: 8 B–K2 B–N2 9 BxN BxB 10 PxP PxP (10 . . . QBxP gives White too great a superiority in the center.) 11 0–0 Q–Q3 12 R–B1 P–R3 13 P–QR3 N–Q2 14 P–QN4 P–QN4 15 N–K1 (15 N–Q2! and 16 N–N3 would keep White's slight advantage.) 15 . . . P–B3 16 N–Q3 N–N3? (16 . . . P–QR4! equalizes.) 17 P–QR4! B–Q1 18 N–B5 B–B1 19 P–R5 B–B2 20 P–N3 N–B5 21 P–K4! B–R6 22 R–K1 PxP 23 N/3xKP Q–N3 24 B–R5! Q–R2 25 Q–B3 P–B4? (25 . . . Q–B4 is required for defensive purposes.) 26 N–B3 P–N3 27 QxQBP PxB 28 N–Q5 P–B5 29 R–K7 Q–B4 30 RxB QR–K1 31 QxKRP R–B2 32 RxR KxR 33 QxBP R–K7 34 Q–B7ch K–B1 35 N–B4 Black resigns.

8 . . . NxP!

It is imperative to exchange off a pair of minor pieces, as this makes Black's defensive task considerably easier. Inferior is 8 . . . PxP?! (as played by Tartakower in 1922), since after 9 B–Q3! Black has no compensation for his weakened Queenside. Whether Black plays 9 . . . B–N2 or 9 . . . B–K3, White has excellent prospects both along the QB–file and with a timely N–K5.

9 BxB

After 9 B–N3 B–N2! the Bishop reaches the desired central diagonal, and Black will have no problems in equalizing.

9 . . . QxB

The only correct capture. 9 . . . NxN? 10 BxQ NxQ 11 B–K7
B–K1 12 B–R3 leads to a trapped Knight, whereas 9 . . . NxB?!
places the Knight in an inactive position and allows White a clear
central superiority after, e.g., 10 B–K2 B–N2 10 0–0 N–Q2 12
Q–R4 P–R3 13 KR–Q1.

10 NxN!

It is absolutely necessary to give Black a permanent weakness—
here the QP. After the routine 10 B–Q3 B–N2 Black is O.K.

10 . . . PxN

DIAGRAM 31

BLACK

WHITE

*Queen's Gambit Declined
after 10 . . . P×N*

A critical position for the evaluation of the whole Tartakower
Variation. Black's Kingside has been developed long since and, if
he succeeds in smoothly developing his Queenside, then he is
assured of full equality. If White continues inexactly, then the
position can easily turn against him. Witness the course of the
game M. Bertok–R. Fischer, Stockholm Interzonal 1962: 11 B–K2
B–K3! 12 0–0 P–QB4 13 PxP? (13 N–K5 keeps equality.) 13 . . .
PxP 14 Q–R4 Q–N2! 15 Q–R3 N–Q2 16 N–K1 P–QR4 17
N–Q3 P–B5 18 N–B4 KR–N1, and the pressure along the QN–file

gives Black some advantage. Fischer went on to win after 19 QR–N1? (Necessary is 19 NxB PxN   20 B–N4 R–R3   21 P–QN3!.) 19 . . . B–B4!   20 QR–Q1 N–B3   21 R–Q2 P–N4!   22 NxP NxN 23 BxP B–K3   24 KR–Q1?! NxP!   25 QxN BxB   26 P–KR4 R–K1 27 Q–KN3 Q–K2   28 P–N3 B–K3   29 P–B4 P–N5   30 P–R5 Q–B4ch   31 R–B2 B–B4 White resigns.

11 R–B1!

Immediately exerting pressure on Black's weakened Queenside. White need not fear 11 . . . Q–N5ch?, since after 12 Q–Q2 QxQch 13 KxQ! White's King is quite safe in the center while his pressure along the QB–file is close to unbearable.

11 . . . B–K3

To solve his Queenside problems, Black must soon get in . . . P–QB4 and, to play this, the QP must be protected. The QB is better placed on K3 than on QN2 for two reasons: (1) the QB1–KR6 diagonal is open, whereas the QR1–KR8 diagonal is blocked by the QP, and (2) Black's Queen will be able to make good use of the QN2 square.

12 Q–R4!?

White sees that 12 . . . P–QB4 is coming, and, since it cannot be prevented, White tries to establish play against Black's QBP once it has reached its fourth rank. The text move is an idea of grandmaster Salo Flohr, and, since its introduction in the early 1930's, it has constituted the main line of the Tartakower Variation.

Nevertheless, the Queen maneuver takes time, and after the Queen lands on its destined QR3 square it is hardly well placed there. Therefore the developmental—though less popular—12 B–Q3! is more likely to lead to the slight opening edge White has every reason to expect in the QGD. A logical continuation would be 12 . . . P–QB4   13 PxP PxP   14 0–0 N–Q2   15 P–K4! PxP   16 BxP QR–N1   17 P–QN3 KR–B1   18 R–K1, with the superior Queenside pawn formation and active piece placement giving White the slightly better middlegame prospects.

12 . . . P–QB4

Since this is the way in which Black plans to free his position, there is absolutely no reason not to play this move here.

13 Q–R3

The idea behind White's previous move. Since Black's QBP is pinned, White exerts definite pressure against it, requiring very exact play from his opponent. The text is much more flexible than 13 PxP PxP 14 Q–R3.

13 . . . R–B1

The only satisfactory way of protecting the pawn. After 13 . . . N–Q2?! 14 B–R6 Black will have difficulty on the Queenside.

We shall now follow R. Fischer–B. Spassky, 1972 World Championship Match, Game #6:

14 B–N5!?

DIAGRAM 32

BLACK

WHITE

Fischer–Spassky 1972
Game 6
after 14 B–N5!?

An interesting, though very double-edged, plan. White tries to make it more difficult for Black to complete the development of his Queenside, but risks his Bishop being caught in an awkward situation. Safer is 14 B–K2, after which Black's best idea is to regroup with 14 . . . Q–N2!, leading to approximate equality after 15 PxP PxP 16 0–0 Q–N3 17 R–B3 N–Q2 18 KR–B1 R/B–N1.

14 . . . P–R3?!

A serious loss of time, since it carries no threat. Here too the most effective plan is 14 . . . Q–N2!, and after 15 PxP PxP   16 RxP RxR 17 QxR N–R3!   18 BxN QxB Black's edge in development is full compensation for the pawn, and White does best to head for a draw with 19 Q–R3 Q–B5   20 Q–B3.

15 PxP! PxP

15 . . . RxP?! is met by the simple 16 0–0 parrying Black's threats while retaining the superior pawn formation.

16 0–0 R–R2?!

The Rook does not stand well here; therefore it was better to chase back the Bishop by 16 . . . Q–N2 or 16 . . . Q–R2.

17 B–K2 N–Q2?!

Running into another unpleasant pin. The minor evil is 17 . . . P–B5, even though it does give White's Knight a great square on Q4.

18 N–Q4!

Making it extremely difficult for Black to come up with a satisfactory plan. If, for instance, 18 . . . N–B3, then 19 N–N3! N–Q2   20 R–B3!, followed by 21 KR–B1 exerting very strong pressure on the QBP. Still, this would have been better than what happens in the game.

18 . . . Q–B1?

Unpinning the Queen, but after. . .

19 NxB! PxN   20 P–K4!

. . .the looseness of Black's position is alarming.

20 . . . P–Q5?

A protected passed pawn is great to have—in the endgame! Here it leads to the final breaking up of Black's position, since White's pieces—particularly the Bishop—will now attain open lines against Black's King.

21 P-B4! Q-K2 22 P-K5 R-N1 23 B-B4 K-R1 24 Q-R3!

Fischer is a virtuoso in playing both sides of the board. After 24 . . . RxP 25 BxKP the advance of White's KP and KBP will be decisive. Of course, what happens in the game is no better for Black.

24 . . . N-B1 25 P-QN3! P-QR4 26 P-B5! PxP 27 RxP N-R2 28 QR-B1 Q-Q1 29 Q-N3 R-K2 30 P-KR4

Taking the KN4 square away from the Knight.

30 . . . R/1-N2 31 P-K6!

Making it possible for the Queen to get to K5.

31 . . . R/N-B2 32 Q-K5 Q-K1 33 P-R4

Here, and over the next few moves, Fischer marks time to demonstrate the inherent helplessness of Black's position.

33 . . . Q-Q1 34 R/1-B2 Q-K1 35 R/2-B3 Q-Q1 36 B-Q3 Q-K1 37 Q-K4!

The beginning of the end. The threat is 38 R-B8ch!, e.g., 37 . . . RxP 38 R-B8ch! NxR 39 RxNch QxR 40 Q-R7mate.

37 . . . N-B3 38 RxN!

DIAGRAM 33

BLACK

WHITE

Fischer–Spassky 1972
Game 6
after 38 R × N!

The denuding of Black's Kingside leads to a rapid finish.

38 . . . PxR   39 RxP K–N1   40 B–B4 K–R1   41 Q–B4 Black resigns

The threat is 42 R–B8ch, and 41 . . . K–N1   42 QxRP leaves Black defenseless against 43 R–N6ch R–KN2   44 P–K7ch.

CHAPTER 9

Bad Moves: How Not to Play Them

The two general approaches in aiming for success—in business, politics, life, chess—are the positive approach and the non-negative one. The really great achievers are those who think positively, of course, going out and making their own successes. This is the best approach in chess also, and that is why this book bears the positive title "How to Play Good Opening Moves." That doesn't mean, however, that the non-negative approach should be derided. Many people achieve perfectly satisfactory results by going along with the tide, never rocking the boat, keeping their noses clean and just not doing anything wrong.

In chess, if you don't do anything really wrong, you will come out quite well at the end. True, you won't win all your games, but the pleasant combination of many wins and some draws will always ensure a high tournament placing. The purpose of this chapter is to help you avoid bad moves—so that there will be opportunities for good ones later on. *The* principal way to avoid bad moves is to play in accordance with the opening principles that we have discussed. If a move does not further at least one of the opening goals, chances are high that it will turn out to be a bad move. A helpful corollary in weeding out bad moves is to play in accordance with the basic objectives of the particular opening chosen.

A classical example of what not to do is shown in the brilliant attacking miniature P. Morphy–Duke of Brunswick and Count Isouard, Paris 1858, Philidor's Defense:

1 P–K4 P–K4   2 N–KB3 P–Q3   3 P–Q4 B–N5?

The basic idea of the somewhat cramping Philidor's Defense is to protect the KP with 3 . . . N–Q2 or the more modern 3 . . . N–KB3! 4 N–B3 QN–Q2. The indirect defense of the pawn by pinning the Knight is shown to be inferior on the very next move!

4 PxP! BxN

Forced, as otherwise a pawn is lost.

5 QxB PxP   6 B–QB4 N–KB3?

The "Allies" do see the threat of mate in one, but don't see White's next move. Necessary is 6 . . . Q–K2.

7 Q–QN3!

The double threat against KB2 and QN7 wins material.

7 . . . Q–K2   8 N–B3!?

Morphy by now realizes the "strength" of his opponents and has no interest in the endgame after 8 QxP Q–N5ch or the superior, but somewhat complicated, middlegame after 8 BxPch QxB 9 QxP. He is sure that sound, rapid development will lead to an even faster win.

8 . . . P–B3   9 B–KN5 P–N4?

The creation of new weaknesses when already well behind in development is usually equivalent to suicide. The Queenside had to be developed with the ugly looking 9 . . . N–R3.

10 NxP! PxN   11 BxNPch QN–Q2   12 0–0–0

Castling with a gain of time. When this game ends all of White's pieces will have had a role in his victory, whereas Black's Kingside pieces will just have stood by, playing the role of spectators to the action on the Queenside and in the center.

12 . . . R–Q1   13 RxN! RxR   14 R–Q1 Q–K3   15 BxRch! NxB 16 Q–N8ch!! NxQ   17 R–Q8mate

Ah, but you say: "That was over a hundred years ago, and the World Champion was playing against two amateurs." Yes, but, as

DIAGRAM 34

BLACK

WHITE

Morphy–"Allies"
after 9 . . . P–N4?

I mentioned earlier, we present–day masters are also afflicted with the disease of playing bad moves, because we think we see exceptions to the basic principles when in fact exceptions do not exist. In the examples to follow, I have used only recent master–level play. The point throughout is "How *not* to play bad moves."

1: *If your move is contrary to the spirit of the opening variation—this will be bad.*
Example: A Karpov–A. Lutikov, Moscow 1979, Center Counter Defense:

1 P–K4 P–Q4 2 PxP QxP 3 N–QB3 Q–Q3?

The Center Counter is in itself a shade inferior. In any case, required is 3 . . . Q–QR4, so that the Queen will be safe and will immobilize White's QN by the pin resulting after 4 P–Q4. On Q3 the Queen is nothing but vulnerable.

4 P–Q4 N–KB3 5 N–B3 P–QR3 6 B–K3 N–B3 7 Q–Q2 B–N5 8 N–KN5! P–K4?

Allowing a cramping pawn on Q5 is plainly stupid. The modest 8 . . . P–K3 was in order.

9 P–Q5! N–N5 10 P–B3 B–B4 11 KN–K4

Gaining time by attacking the misplaced Queen.

**11 . . . Q–Q2   12 0–0–0 P–B3   13 PxP! QxQch   14 RxQ BxN?!
15 NxB NxBP(3)   16 NxNch PxN   17 B–Q3**

Superior pawn structure, better development and the Bishop
pair in an open position—the combination of these advantages
allows Karpov to drive Black into a hopeless situation very quickly.

**17 . . . 0–0–0   18 KR–Q1 K–B2   19 P–B3 P–KR4   20 B–KB5
RxR   21 RxR N–N1   22 P–KR4 B–R3   23 BxB RxB   24 P–R4 R–R1
25 P–QN4! P–N3   26 P–N5 R–N1   27 K–B2 PxP   28 PxP R–K1
29 P–QB4 Black resigns.**

2: *If you leave your pawns unprotected—this will be bad.*
Example: E. Sveshnikov–Buljovcic, Novi Sad 1979, KB Fianchetto
Opening:

**1 P–KN3 P–QB4   2 B–N2 N–KB3   3 N–KB3 P–KN3   4 P–B3
B–N2   5 P–Q4 0–0?**

Castling is a fine goal, of course, but pawns shouldn't be left
hanging. Correct are 5 . . . PxP or 5 . . . Q–N3.

6 PxP! Q–B2   7 P–QN4!

Black expected that he could recover the pawn easily, but it
turns out otherwise.

**7 . . . P–QR4   8 B–B4! Q–B3   9 0–0 PxP   10 PxP Q–N4   11
P–QR3 N–B3   12 N–B3 Q–B5   13 N–QR4 N–Q4   14 N–Q2 Q–Q5
15 BxN! QxR   16 Q–N3!**

To get back his "sacrificed" pawn, Black has had to neglect his
development and compromise his Queenside. By a true Exchange
sacrifice White gains the necessary time to exploit Black's
weaknesses.

**16 . . . Q–B3   17 N–K4 Q–B4   18 N–N6 R–R2   19 P–QR4!
B–K4   20 BxB NxB   21 P–B4 N–B3   22 R–Q1 P–R4   23 N–N5
P–K3   24 B–N2 P–K4   25 B–K4 Q–B3   26 R–Q6 N–Q5   27 RxQ
NxQ   28 B–Q5 K–N2   29 PxP N–Q5   30 BxBP Black resigns**

As can be seen, Black is still playing without his QR and QB!

3: *If you weaken your King position — this will be bad.*

A) Example with King in the center: V. Jansa–J. Arnason, Polonica Zdroj 1979, Ruy Lopez:

1 P-K4 P-K4   2 N-KB3 N-QB3   3 B-N5 P-QR3   4 B-R4 P-Q3
5 0-0 B-Q2   6 R-K1 KN-K2   7 P-B3 P-R3   8 P-Q4

DIAGRAM 35

BLACK

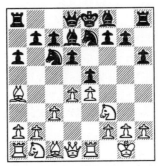

WHITE

Jansa–Arnason 1979
after 8 P-Q4

Black has chosen the safe but passive Steinitz Deferred variation, the primary aim of which is to safeguard (or overprotect) K4. In conformity with this idea, the next move should be 8 . . . N-N3. Instead. . .

8 . . . P-KN4?

None of Black's pieces are set for an attack, and White has no Kingside weaknesses. Thus Black's "attack" has no chance for success, and the only legacy of the text move will be a chronic weakening of his own King position.

9 PxP!

Opening the position to be able to take future advantage of Black's self-created weakness.

9 . . . PxP   10 QN-Q2 N-N3   11 N-B1 P-N4?!

This weakening of the Queenside means that Black's King will be safe on neither wing.

12 B–B2 P–KN5 13 N/3–Q2 Q–R5 14 N–K3 B–QB4 15 P–KN3 Q–R6 16 N–N3 B–N3 17 B–Q3! N/B–K2 18 B–B1 Q–R4 19 P–KR3!

Black's Kingside weaknesses are coming home to roost.

19 . . . BxN 20 BxB R–Q1 21 N–B5 B–B1 22 Q–K2 R–N1 23 NxP!

Black's Queenside weaknesses are also coming home to roost. Of course, 23 . . . BxN? allows 24 PxP.

23 . . . N–B5 24 BxN BxN 25 B–K3 R–Q3 26 QR–Q1 P–N5 27 P–QB4 B–N2 28 B–B5 N–B3 29 BxR PxB 30 P–B5 PxP 31 Q–N5 B–R1 32 P–KR4 K–B1 33 QxPch K–N2 34 R–Q7 Q–N3 35 B–B4 R–KB1 36 R–Q6 N–Q5 37 RxQch Black resigns

B) Example with castled King: A. Groszpeter–L. Hazai, 1979 Hungarian Championship, Ruy Lopez, Open Variation:

1 P–K4 P–K4 2 N–KB3 N–QB3 3 B–N5 P–QR3 4 B–R4 N–B3 5 0–0 NxP 6 P–Q4 P–QN4 7 B–N3 P–Q4 8 PxP B–K3 9 QN–Q2 N–B4 10 P–B3 B–N5 11 P–KR3 B–R4 12 P–KN4?

Why this horrible weakening of the Kingside? With Black's King still in the center White's KP is safe anyway, and correct is 12 B–B2 (12 . . . NxP? 13 Q–K1!).

12 . . . B–N3 13 N–Q4 NxN 14 PxN N–K3 15 P–B4 B–Q6! 16 R–B3 B–B5 17 N–B1 P–QB4 18 BxB?

Just increases Black's central influence. After the developmental 18 B–K3! Black's advantage would be small.

18 . . . NPxB! 19 PxP?! BxPch 20 K–N2 P–KR4!

Simple but strong: Black takes advantage of 12 P–KN4?.

21 Q–R4ch K–B1 22 P–N5 P–N3 23 P–R4 Q–B1! 24 B–K3 R–QN1 25 R–N1 P–Q5 26 B–B2 R–N5 27 Q–B2 Q–N2?

Winning was 27 . . . Q–B3!. After the text White could defend with 28 N–Q2!.

28 P-B5? P-Q6 29 BxBch NxB 30 Q-B2 N-K5 31 Q-Q4 P-B6! 32 QxQP RxPch 33 RxR PxR 34 P-B6 K-N1 35 Q-Q8ch K-R2 36 Q-K7 P-N8 = Q White resigns

4: *If you pay insufficient attention to the center—this will be bad.*
Example: A. Groszpeter–M. Suba, Kecskemet 1979, Alekhine's Defense.

1 P-K4 N-KB3 2 N-QB3

In order to secure an advantage 2 P-K5 is required.

2 . . . P-Q4 3 P-K5 KN-Q2 4 NxP?!

The liquidation of the center pawns means that White is left with dead equality. Instead, logical is 4 P-Q4, leading to a variation of the French Defense if Black plays 4 . . . P-K3.

4 . . . NxP 5 N-K3 P-QB4 6 P-QN3?

White's Q4 is in Black's hands and there is little to be done about it. Therefore, correct is 6 P-KN3!, followed by 7 B-N2, establishing control over Q5 and preparing Kingside castling.

6 . . . N/K-B3! 7 B-N2 P-K4!

Black has a firm grip on his Q5 and K4 squares—and the advantage.

8 P-N3 B-Q3 9 B-N2 0-0 10 N-K2 P-B4 11 N-QB4 B-B2 12 P-Q3 B-K3

Black is better because he has the superior central influence and no disadvantages. White should now play 13 N-B3! to contest the key Q5 square. After the text move White gets ground down in the center.

13 Q-Q2? B-Q4! 14 BxB QxB 15 0-0-0 N-Q5 16 N-K3 Q-Q2 17 N-B3 N/1-B3 18 K-N1 P-QN4! 19 R/Q-KB1 B-R4 20 P-B4 QR-K1! 21 Q-B2 PxP 22 PxP R-B2 23 R/R-N1 N-N5 24 R-N3 B-Q1! 25 Q-N2 B-R5 26 R-R3 R/2-K2! 27 N/B-Q1 N/NxBP!

Because of Black's bind in the center, the position has become ripe for a decisive combination. If now 28 BxN, Black wins with 28

DIAGRAM 36

BLACK

WHITE

Goszpeter–Suba
Kecskemet 1979
after 12 . . . B–K3

. . . N–R6ch!   29 K–N2 QxBch   30 KxN RxN!   31 RxR P–N5ch 32 K–R4 Q–Q2ch   33 K–R5 B–Q1ch, followed by mate soon.

28 NxN R–K7   29 QxR NxQ   30 RxB QxP   31 R–K1 P–B5   32 B–K5 PxP   33 PxP QxPch   34 N–N2 R–Q1!   35 N–R1 N–B6ch   36 BxN QxB   37 R–QB1 Q–B6   38 N–B2 R–Q7   39 R–K1 RxN!   40 R–K8ch K–B2 White resigns

5: *If you develop your pieces away from the center—this will be bad.*
Example: V. Hort–M. Stean, Amsterdam 1979, Sicilian Defense, Closed Variation:

1 P–KB4 P–KN3   2 P–KN3 B–N2   3 B–N2 P–QB4   4 P–K4 N–QB3

By transposition of moves, something like the Closed Variation of the Sicilian Defense has arisen. If White now plays 5 N–QB3 or 5 P–Q3 everything would be "normal." However:

5 N–KR3? P–Q4!

In the Sicilian Defense, if Black gets in this thematic advance he has at least equality. If 6 PxP?! BxN!   7 BxB QxP and Black has a clear advantage. Belatedly, but correctly, Hort starts paying attention to the center.

6 N–B3!? PxP 7 NxP N–B3 8 NxNch BxN 9 N–B2 B–N2 10 0–0 0–0 11 P–Q3 Q–B2 12 P–B3 P–N3 13 B–Q2 B–N2 14 P–QR3 QR–Q1

The legacy of White's 5th move is that Black has greater central influence and therefore some advantage. With careful defense White is just able to hold: 15 Q–R4! N–R4 16 BxB QxB 17 QR–Q1 Q–Q2 18 Q–B2 Q–B3 19 N–K4 R–Q2 20 B–K3 KR–Q1 21 P–B5 PxP! 22 RxP Q–K3?! (22 . . . N–B5! retains a slight edge.) 23 R–B3! Q–N6 24 QxQ NxQ 25 N–B2 Draw.

6: *If you move the same piece twice and its second move is away from the center—this will be bad.*
Example A: L. Portisch–B. Ivkov, Rio de Janeiro Interzonal 1979, Queen's Gambit Declined, Exchange Variation.

1 P–Q4 P–Q4 2 P–QB4 P–K3 3 N–QB3 B–K2 4 PxP PxP 5 B–B4 P–QB3 6 P–K3 B–KB4 7 KN–K2 N–Q2 8 N–N3 B–N3 9 B–K2

DIAGRAM 37

BLACK

WHITE

Portisch–Ivkov
Rio De Janiero 1979
after 9 B–K2

The Exchange Variation has so far been handled in a slightly unusual way, but after the routine 9 . . . KN–B3, Black would have a satisfactory position.

9 . . . N–B1?

With the idea of playing 10 . . . N–K3. However, White is able to exploit Black's "undevelopment" with the following sharp sacrifice.

10 P–KR4!! BxP 11 Q–N3! BxN 12 BxB Q–N3 13 Q–R3!

His open lines and active development give White more than sufficient compensation for the relatively unimportant KRP. With perfect defense Black could hold, but in practice such positions are usually lost. The game continued: 13 . . . N–K2 14 N–R4 Q–Q1 15 N–B5 Q–N3 16 N–R4 Q–Q1 17 N–B5 Q–N3 18 B–K5! P–B3 19 B–R2 B–B2 (Perhaps better is 19 . . . K–B2!?.) 20 B–Q6! N/1–N3 21 B–Q3! N–QB1 22 B–N3 P–QR4 23 0–0 N/N–K2 24 KR–K1 R–R2 25 Q–B3 P–R5?! (Better is 25 . . . Q–N5.) 26 QR–N1 Q–Q1?! 27 B–N8! P–QN4 28 BxR NxB 29 P–QN3 PxP 30 PxP 0–0 31 R–R1 N/K–B1 32 B–B5 R–K1 33 R–R6 Q–B2 34 R/K–R1 R–K2 35 N–Q3 B–K1 36 Q–B5 Q–N2 37 N–N4 R–QB2 38 B–K6ch B–B2 39 BxN NxB 40 RxP RxR 41 NxR Black resigns.

Example B: C. Partos–V. Korchnoi, Biel 1979, Old Benoni Defense:

1 P–Q4 N–KB3 2 P–QB4 P–B4 3 P–Q5 P–K4 4 N–QB3 P–Q3 5 P–K4 P–KN3 6 P–KR3 N–R4?

Why, oh, why? Correct are the usual moves, 6 . . . B–N2 or 6 . . . QN–Q2.

7 B–K3! B–N2 8 B–K2 Q–N3 9 P–R3! N–B5?! 10 B–B3 B–Q2 11 R–N1 Q–R3?! 12 P–KN3 N–R4 13 B–K2 0–0 14 N–N5!

White has a significant space advantage, and Black's pieces stand awkwardly on both sides of the board. Realizing that normal play offers few prospects, Korchnoi goes for complications and scores a lucky win: 14 . . . P–B4!? 15 PxP BxP 16 R–B1 N–Q2!? 17 P–KN4 B–K5 18 R–R2 N–B5 19 P–B3 BxBP 20 NxB P–K5 21 N–N5 BxP 22 N–K6! NxB 23 KxN BxR 24 QxB N–K4 25

Q–B3 (25 Q–B2! is a simpler win.) 25 . . . R–B6! 26 R–B2! RxP 27 R–B4? (27 NxBP! wins) 27 . . . Q–R5 28 RxP?? (28 NxQP is good enough for a draw.) 28 . . . R–R8 29 Q–Q2 Q–N6! 30 N–B3 NxBP 31 Q–R2 QxN 32 QxN Q–N7ch! 33 K–B3 R–R6ch White resigns.

7: *If you waste time—this will be bad.*
Example: R. Rodriguez–L. Ljubojevic, Riga Interzonal 1979, Queen's Gambit Declined, Tarrasch Defense.

1 P–QB4 P–QB4 2 N–KB3 N–KB3 3 N–B3 P–K3 4 P–K3 P–Q4 5 PxP PxP 6 P–Q4 N–B3 7 B–K2 N–K5!?

Moving the same piece twice, *but* towards the center. By transposition of moves, we have reached the Tarrasch Defense to the QGD, where, instead of fianchettoing his KB, White has played P–K3 and B–K2. This set-up is less dangerous for Black.

8 0–0 B–K2 9 P–KR3?

Weakens the Kingside while wasting time. Approximate equality is retained by 9 PxP NxN 10 PxN BxP 11 P–B4.

9 . . . 0–0 10 B–Q3?

Why move the KB again? If White wanted to put the Bishop on Q3, he could have played 7 B–Q3.

10 . . . B–B4! 11 PxP BxBP 12 N–QR4 B–K2 13 P–QN3 Q–Q3! 14 B–N2 Q–N3 15 N–K1 BxP! 16 P–B3

In the game Black played 16 . . . QR–Q1?!, which only retained a slight edge in a subsequent endgame (17 Q–K2 N–N6 18 BxQ NxQch), and, after some later blunders, Black even lost. A winning position was to be had with 16 . . . B–R5! (threatening 17 . . . BxN.) 17 Q–K2 N–N6! 18 BxQ NxQch 19 K–R2 B–K3!, with Black a pawn up and standing beautifully.

8: *If you create unnecessary weaknesses—this will be bad.*
Example: P. Popovic–S. Marjanovic, Yugoslavia 1979, Sicilian Defense.

1 P–K4 P–QB4 2 N–KB3 P–Q3 3 N–B3 P–QR3 4 P–KN3 N–QB3 5 B–N2 P–KN3 6 P–Q4! PxP 7 NxP B–Q2 8 N–Q5 P–K3?

DIAGRAM 38

BLACK

WHITE

Rodriguez–Ljubojevic
Riga 1979
after 16 P–B3

Since Black will fianchetto the KB, this leads to a frightfully weak QP. Correct is the normal 8 . . . B–N2, and, after 9 B–K3, 9 . . . R–B1.

9 N–K3 Q–B2   10 0–0 B–N2   11 NxN! PxN   12 N–B4!

The damage wrought by Black's 8th move is now obvious. The attempt to protect the QP by advancing it fails to White's brilliant sacrifice, made possible by White's huge lead in development.

12 . . . P–Q4   13 PxP BPxP   14 BxP! R–Q1

Black is defenseless after 14 . . . PxB   15 QxP—not that what happens now is much better.

15 B–B4 Q–B4   16 N–Q6ch K–K2   17 P–B4!! PxB   18 N–N7 QxQBP   19 R–B1 Q–N4   20 R–K1ch B–K3   21 R–B7ch K–K1   22 RxP!! B–B3   23 R–B7 Q–N3   24 Q–N4 N–K2   25 RxB Q–Q5   26 NxR Black resigns

9: *If you greedily hang on to material—this will be bad.*
Example: G. Sosonso–R. Hübner, Tilburg 1979, Catalan Opening.

1 P–Q4 N–KB3   2 P–QB4 P–K3   3 P–KN3 P–Q4   4 B–N2 PxP   5 N–KB3 P–QR3   6 0–0! P–QN4?!

It is generally well recognized that in open positions King safety is of paramount importance. Therefore, grabbing stray pawns or holding on to gambit pawns is foolhardy when the position requires castling. However, positions which *appear* to be closed can also quickly spring to life if the opponent has an edge in development such as White has here. Black's attempt at retaining the QBP meets with a violent refutation. In order are moves such as 6 . . . P-B4 or 6 . . . N-B3, and the modest 6 . . . B-K2 also is reasonable.

7 N-K5! N-Q4   8 N-QB3! P-QB3?   9 NxN! KPxP   10 P-K4! B-K3   11 P-QR4! P-N5   12 PxP! BxP?!

White has steadfastly tried to open the position as much as possible. Black, for his part, must try to keep it as closed as possible. Therefore, 12 . . . PxP is required, even though White then has the option of recovering the sacrificed pawn immediately with 13 NxQBP.

13 Q-N4!

DIAGRAM 39

BLACK

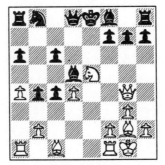

WHITE

Sosonko–Hübner
Tilburg 1979
after 13 Q–N4

White has a winning attack, since 13 . . . BxB is met by 14 R–K1! and 13 . . . B–K3 by 14 Q–R5 B–K2   15 NxQBP/6.

13 . . . P-KR4 14 BxB!! PxB 15 Q-B5 R-QR2 16 R-K1 R-K2
17 B-N5 P-N3 18 BxR Black resigns

10: *If you muddle around—this will be bad.*
Example: V. Smyslov-L. Portisch, Tilburg 1979, Sicilian Defense,
Najdorf Variation.

1 P-K4 P-QB4 2 N-KB3 P-Q3 3 P-Q4 PxP 4 NxP N-KB3 5
N-QB3 P-QR3 6 B-KN5 P-K3 7 Q-K2?

The idea behind the sharp 6 B-KN5 is to follow up with the
central and developmental 7 P-B4, 8 Q-B3 and 9 0-0-0. This text
does nothing for the center and inhibits the development of the KB.

7 . . . P-R3 8 B-R4 B-K2 9 B-N3?

White prevents the equalizing 9 . . . NxP! that would follow 9
0-0-0, but in doing so incurs an inferior position instead.

9 . . . P-K4! 10 N-N3 P-QN4! 11 P-B4 0-0 12 Q-Q3?

DIAGRAM 40

BLACK

WHITE

Smyslov-Portisch
Tilburg 1979
after 12 Q-Q3?

What has White accomplished with his opening play? It has
taken the QB three moves to wind up on KN3, the Queen has
expended two moves to stand awkwardly on Q3, and the KN has

been shunted to inactivity at QN3. Black has completed Kingside development, started thematic Queenside play and has a foothold in the center. Already Black is considerably better, and in the further course of the game he expands his advantage. White, of course, should have followed up 11 P–B4 with the consistent 12 PxP.

Black won as follows: 12 . . . QN–Q2   13 B–K2 B–N2   14 0–0 R–B1   15 QR–Q1 Q–B2   16 P–QR3 N–N3   17 N–Q2 N/B–Q2   18 B–N4 QR–Q1   19 BxN RxB   20 K–R1 B–KB3   21 Q–K3 R–K1   22 B–B2 N–R5!   23 NxN PxN   24 P–B3 PxP   25 QxP P–Q4   26 QxQ RxQ   27 B–N3 R/B–K2   28 PxP BxQP   29 R/Q–K1 R–K7   30 RxR RxR   31 R–B2 RxR   32 BxR B–N4   33 B–K1 B–K6   34 P–B4 B–K3   35 N–B1 B–R2   36 B–B3 BxP   37 N–N3 B–Q6   38 N–R5 P–B3   39 P–R3 K–B2   40 K–R2 B–N1ch   41 P–N3 B–N3   42 N–B4 B–K5   43 K–N1 P–N4   44 N–R5 B–R2ch   45 K–B1 P–B4   46 N–B6 B–B3   47 P–R4 B–B4   48 K–K2 K–N3   49 PxP PxP   50 K–K1 P–N5   51 B–K5 B–K2   52 N–N8 B–KN4   53 B–B4 B–Q1   54 B–Q6 K–B2   55 N–R6ch K–K3   56 B–B4 B–B3   57 B–B1 B–Q4 White resigns.

CHAPTER 10
Castling: Early or Late?

Rapid castling is one of the primary goals of sound opening strategy. *You should try to castle quickly.* Castling brings the following three major benefits: (1) the King is safe, (2) the castled Rook is brought closer to potential action, and (3) central activity is furthered, both because the King is out of the way and because the castled Rook can be utilized. In general, these two guidelines apply:

(1) Rapid castling is more critical for Black than for White.
(2) Open positions—particularly those resulting from 1 P–K4 —call for quicker castling than closed positions.

It cannot be overstressed that in open positions the side with the uncastled King suffers from two serious problems: (1) his King position prevents the execution of otherwise logical plans, and (2) his King is inherently unsafe. Let us illustrate the first problem with a few simple examples. You are White, and the game has opened as follows: 1 P–K4 P–QB4 2 N–KB3 P–K3 3 P–Q4 PxP 4 NxP N–KB3. Black is menacing the KP, and it would be nice to be able to play 5 P–K5, safeguarding the pawn while attacking Black's Knight. Yet 5 P–K5 is an error, because with 5 . . . Q–R4 *check* Black captures the pawn for nothing. However, if White had been castled, then P–K5 would be both safe and strong.

Or consider a position commonly arising from the Exchange Variation of the Ruy Lopez: 1 P–K4 P–K4 2 N–KB3 N–QB3 3 B–N5 P–QR3 4 BxN QPxB 5 0–0!. The early commercial chess

computers invariably played 5 . . . N–B3, and after 6 NxP, 6
. . . Q–Q5?! with a double attack on the Knight and KP. And
after 7 N–KB3, Black played 7 . . . QxKP??, noticing, *always
too late*, that, instead of recovering the pawn Black loses his
Queen to 8 R–K1.

The so-called Fool's Mates—ending the game in two, three or
four moves—are based on the fact that the King in the center is
vulnerable to sudden attacks. In open positions, the King
remains vulnerable for a long time, even if no immediate
disaster occurs. The King's inherent vulnerability is well
illustrated by the game E. Mednis–E. Ermenkov, New York
International 1980, Sicilian Defense, Taimanov Variation:

**1 P–K4 P–QB4   2 N–KB3 N–QB3   3 P–Q4 PxP   4 NxP P–K3
5 N–N5 P–Q3   6 P–QB4 N–B3   7 N/1–B3 P–QR3   8 N–R3 B–K2
9 B–K2 P–QN3**

We have entered one of the main lines of the Taimanov
Variation. White has some spatial advantage, yet Black's
position is sound and solid. Black's usual move is 9 . . . 0–0,
though the immediate fianchetto of the QB looks playable.

10 0–0 B–N2   11 B–K3 N–K4

Instead 11 . . . 0–0 transposes back into known lines. By
delaying castling, Black plays with fire.

12 P–B4! N/4–Q2   13 B–B3 Q–B2?!

Why doesn't Black castle?

14 Q–K2 R–QN1?!

Again, there is no reason not to castle.

15 QR–B1 P–R3?!

Only after this move did it become clear to me why the
Bulgarian GM has avoided castling: he wants to leave his King in
the center and attack my King. However, this plan should *not*
prove successful. White's Kingside has no weaknesses, and the
subsequent opening of the position will expose Black's King. With
my 16th move I safeguard my King further, and with my 17th
move I start to counterattack.

16 K–R1! P–KN4   17 B–R5! PxP?!

It is safer to keep lines closed with 17 . . . NxB   18 QxN N–B3
19 Q–K2 P–N5.

18 QBxKBP N–K4

If 18 . . . Q–B4?, 19 N–Q5!, and after 19 . . . KPxN   20 BPxP!
Q–Q5   21 R–B4 Black's Queen is trapped. Black has good control
of the central squares on his side of the board and thus he thinks he
is safe. White's next shot explodes this myth.

19 N–Q5!!

DIAGRAM 41

BLACK

WHITE

Mednis–Ermenkov
New York 1980
after 19 N–Q5!!

To get at Black's King, lines must be opened and weaknesses
created in the King's vicinity. The Knight sacrifice, followed by 21
BxN!, does this admirably.

19 . . . PxN   20 BPxP! Q–Q1   21 BxN! PxB   22 N–B4 0–0

With the Kingside open, the chances for safety there is slight. Yet
the King is also demonstrably unsafe in the center. Thus 22 . . .
R–QB1 loses to 23 P–Q6! BxQP   24 RxN! QxR (Or 24 . . . RxB   25
R–K6ch! K–B1   26 QxR PxR   27 QxKP) 25 R–B1 Q–K2   26 RxP
QxR   27 BxQch! K–K2   28 Q–N4.

23 NxKP!

23 P–Q6?! recovers the piece, but White wants much more.

23 . . . R–B1   24 QR–Q1! Q–B2

Or 24 . . . B–Q3   25 NxP!, winning, or 24 . . . Q–Q3   25 NxP!
RxN   26 BxRch KxB   27 P–K5, winning.

25 P–Q6! BxQP   26 RxN BxN   27 Q–N4ch K–R2   28 BxP!!

The culmination of White's attack against Black's weakened
King position. There is no defense: a) 28 . . . RxB   29 Q–N6ch; b)
28 . . . BxR   29 Q–N6ch K–R1   30 QxPmate; c) 28 . . . B–B5   29
RxPch! BxR   30 Q–N6ch; d) 28 . . . Q–B8!?   29 Q–B5ch K–N2   30
QxB! R–B4 (30 . . . QxRch   31 R–B1ch) 31 R–N6dbl ch KxB   32
Q–K6mate.

**28 . . . QxB   29 Q–B5ch K–N1   30 RxQ RxR   31 QxB B–B3   32
Q–K6 R/1–B1   33 P–KR3 Black resigns**

Whenever you are in doubt whether to castle, do it—because the
percentages will be in your favor. In any abstract scheme for chess
play early ·castling must be given a high priority. In my con-
sultations for and discussions with programmers of chess computers, I have always stressed the importance of getting the
computer to castle early.

Of course, you as a human being have a mind of your own and
can think independently. Therefore, even though you should
always give high priority to castling, castling should not be done
"automatically." Some of the time castling should be postponed.
We can state this is general terms. *Do not castle if:*

(1) It is unsafe to do so.
(2) There is something better to do.

Since the primary objective of castling is to bring the King into
safety, it is obviously counterproductive to castle into an attack. If
your Kingside is seriously weakened, castling on that side is fraught
with excessive dangers. Even some weakness there should act as a
flag signalling caution. Consider Diagram 42, R. Hübner–V.
Smyslov, Tilburg 1979, after Black's 10th move (1 P–Q4 P–Q4   2

P–QB4 P–QB3 3 N–QB3 N–KB3 4 N–B3 PxP 5 P–QR4 N–R3 6
P–K4 B–N5 7 BxP P–K3 8 B–K3 B–N5 9 Q–B2 QBxN 10 PxB
0–0):

DIAGRAM 42

BLACK

WHITE

Hübner–Smyslov
Tilburg 1979
after Black's 10th move

White has considerable central superiority, a spatial advantage
and two potentially active Bishops. Because of the likelihood that
the position will be opened, White's King will be uncomfortable in
the center. White should castle, yet where? The safer side is the
Queenside, and correct is 11 R–KN1! P–B4 12 B–R6 N–K1 13
P–Q5 N/R–B2 14 0–0–0!, with White having a strong attacking
position and a safe enough King. Instead, the game continued:

11 0–0?!

The King is uncomfortable here for two reasons: (1) the KN
pawn is missing, and (2) there are few defenders nearby (unlike the
situation on the Queenside). There is even another reason why
castling Kingside is inadvisable: White can't take advantage of the
open KN file to attack Black's King.

11 . . . P–B4! 12 P–Q5

After 12 BxN, the *zwischenzug* 12 . . . PxP! equalizes matters.

12 . . . BxN   13 PxB PxP   14 KR–Q1

Now, instead of 14 . . . Q–B1?, 15 PxP, when White's powerful passed QP gave him the advantage (White won on move 30), correct is 14 . . . N–B2. Then, after 15 BxBP R–K1   16 B–K3 (16 Q–R2? loses to 16 . . . N–Q2!   17 BxQP Q–N4ch) 16 . . . R–K4   17 B–B4 R–R4, Black's attacking chances against White's weakened King position give him good prospects in the middlegame.

Just because a King position is not chronically weak, this does not mean that the opponent can't launch a powerful attack against it. The prospect of such a situation should again cause us to delay castling. The course of the opening in R. Vaganian–S. Makarichev, 1979 U.S.S.R. Championship, Queen's Indian Defense is instructive.

1 P–Q4 N–KB3   2 P–QB4 P–K3   3 N–KB3 P–QN3   4 P–QR3 B–N2   5 N–B3 P–Q4   6 PxP NxP   7 P–K3 B–K2   8 B–N5ch P–QB3   9 B–Q3 N–Q2   10 P–K4 NxN   11 PxN P–QB4   12 B–K3

If Black now plays the "logical" 12 . . . 0–0?!, White can launch a strong attack with 13 P–KR4! followed by 14 P–K5, already threatening the sacrifice 15 BxRPch KxB   16 N–N5ch.

12 . . . Q–B2!

A good, flexible, waiting move, making White declare his plans. In the meantime, Black's Queen can find action along the QB file and Black's QR can go to Q1 (and Black could even castle Queenside!).

13 0–0 0–0!

With White's King castled on the Kingside, there are no attacking prospects along the KR–file because such moves as P–KR4 are out of the question. Therefore, Black can complete his Kingside development by castling there. His King is now safe and the position just minimally preferable for White (because of central superiority). Black equalized in due course, but a later error led to a 31–move loss.

If, for the moment, the uncastled King is safe, then it is O.K. to ask if something else should not be accorded higher priority than castling. The "something else" can be either defensive or offensive in nature. For instance, it may well be in order first to prevent the opponent from carrying out a desired defensive maneuver. A good example is the course of the early opening in A. Gipslis–Ruderfer, U.S.S.R. 1979, Giuoco Piano:

1 P–K4 P–K4   2 N–KB3 N–QB3   3 B–B4 B–B4   4 P–B3 N–B3 5 P–Q3 P–Q3   6 QN–Q2 P–QR3

If now the immediate 7 0–0?!, Black replies 7 . . . N–QR4!, exchanges off White's strong KB and obtains ready equality. Therefore, White prevents this possibility.

7 B–N3! 0–0

Of course 7 . . . N–QR4?!   8 B–B2 is fruitless for Black, since White threatens both 9 P–QN4 and the strategic 9 P–Q4.

8 0–0!

Only now—yet note that White still castles quite early!

8 . . . B–R2   9 R–K1 N–K2   10 P–KR3 N–N3   11 N–B1 P–R3 12 N–N3 P–B3   13 P–Q4!

White has prevented Black from exchanging pieces and, due to his central edge, has a clear superiority. White went on to win on move 36.

If one's opponent threatens a course of action which will lead to his advantage, then it becomes even more important to delay castling. Diagram 43, V. Smyslov–O. Romanishin, Tilburg 1979, English Opening, shows the position after 1 P–QB4 P–K4   2 N–QB3 N–KB3   3 N–B3 N–B3   4 P–K3 B–N5   5 Q–B2 BxN   6 QxB Q–K2   7 P–QR3 0–0   8 P–Q3 P–QR4   9 B–K2?! (Better 9 P–QN3.) 9 . . . P–R5.

As a result of White's inaccurate 9th move, Black has succeeded in "fixing" White's Queenside (inhibiting P–QN3 or P–QN4 by White). White's Bishops have very little scope, whereas Black is ready for a central advance with . . . P–Q4. Correct for White now is 10 P–K4!, with the following points: (1) Black's . . . P–Q4 is prevented; (2) White has a strong grip on his Q5; (3) a diagonal is opened for the QB. Instead, White played the automatic and careless 10 0–0?!, after which Black could have gained a slight edge with the thematic 10 . . . P–Q4!   11 PxP NxP   12 Q–B2 B–K3, since in this position Black is more active and controls more space.

DIAGRAM 43

BLACK

WHITE

Smyslov–Romanishin
Tilburg 1979
after 9 . . . P–R5

(Instead he satisfied himself with equality through the modest 10 . . . P–Q3—and still won on move 33.)

Now for some "positive" examples of postponing castling. No one is silly enough to castle when he can mate next move or win the Queen for nothing. Yet there also are less obvious situations where saving the tempo required for castling is in order. How many times have we been exactly one tempo short to achieve the aims of our attack? Many times, of course. Only a very few such instances can be blamed on castling, but it is a factor always to keep in mind. Let us follow the course of the opening in F. Trois–L. Ljubojevic, Buenos Aires 1979, English Opening:

1 P–QB4 P–K4　2 N–QB3 N–QB3　3 P–KN3 P–Q3　4 B–N2 B–K3　5 P–Q3 Q–Q2　6 P–QN4 KN–K2　7 P–N5 N–Q1　8 P–QR4 P–QB3　9 B–QR3

White is very strongly emphasizing the development of his Queenside and consequent pressure against Black's Queenside.

9 . . . P–Q4　10 NPxP NPxP　11 PxP PxP　12 N–B3 P–B3

The net result so far is that White has gained an edge in development, while Black has more pawn influence in the center.

In the game White routinely continued with 13 0–0?!, and in due course had nothing to show for his central inferiority. The consistent course was to work on exploiting his edge in development as follows:

13 P–Q4! P–K5 14 N–Q2

Black's last was forced. White now threatens to get to QB5 via QN3.

14 . . . R–B1 15 N–N5! N/K–B3 16 BxB RxB 17 N–N3 N–N2 18 N–B5! NxN 19 PxN

White has a promising, active position and threatens the immediate 20 N–Q6ch.

Finally, a game in which White demonstrates perfectly the logic of late castling. But please note that it is *White* that does it, and that we have a closed opening.

W. Schmidt–A. Kuligowski
Warsaw Zonal 1979
Benoni Defense

1 P–Q4 N–KB3 2 P–QB4 P–B4 3 P–Q5 P–K3 4 N–QB3 PxP 5 PxP P–Q3 6 P–K4 P–KN3 7 N–B3 B–N2 8 B–KN5 P–KR3 9 B–R4 P–R3 10 N–Q2 P–QN4 11 P–R4!

By undermining Black's Queenside pawn formation, White gets QB4 for his Knight(s).

11 . . . P–N5 12 N/B–N1 Q–K2

The immediate 12 . . . 0–0 looks better.

13 P–B3 P–N4 14 B–B2! 0–0 15 B–K2 QN–Q2 16 N–B4!

Activating both Knights with this and the following move. Black should now exchange one Knight with 16 . . . N–K4.

16 . . . N–R4?! 17 N/1–Q2! N–B5 18 0–0!

The immediate strategic goals have been accomplished, and the KNP needs protection—so White castles!

18 . . . P–B4 19 R–K1 NxBch 20 RxN P–B5 21 P–K5!

DIAGRAM 44

BLACK

WHITE

Schmidt–Kuligowski
Warsaw 1979
after 18 0-0!

This thematic central advance ensures White's advantage. His superior development and Black's positional weaknesses mean that the sacrificed material will be recovered—sooner or later.

21 . . . PxP 22 N–K4! P–QR4 23 R–B1 B–R3 24 R/K–B2! BxN 25 RxB KR–Q1 26 BxP Q–B2 27 B–Q6 N–N3 28 R–B5 R–Q2 29 R–N5 N–B1 30 R–B6??

A tragic time pressure error: White overlooks that after Black's reply he cannot move the attacked Bishop because of 31 . . . QxR. White should have played 30 R–N8!, and after 30 . . . RxR 31 BxR White has Black in an absolute bind and will follow up with the decisive 32 P–Q6!.

30 . . . Q–N3! 31 RxRP RxR 32 RxNch K–B2 33 B–B5 Q–R3! 34 BxP R/RxQP White resigns

At this moment, it may also be worthwhile to go back to the previous chapter and review Portisch–Ivkov, where White castled late, but well, on move 23.

CHAPTER 11
Pawn Play: Center, Formations, Weaknesses

Philidor once referred to the pawns "as the soul of chess." Of course, pawn play is important, yet is only one of a number of key strategems. Still, there is one extremely important aspect of pawn play which does not apply to any other piece: you can't move a pawn backwards! Often you can repair a faulty Queen, Rook, Bishop, Knight or King move by simply moving that piece back where it came from. Not so with a pawn! Therefore, extreme care must be taken before a pawn is touched. Pawn moves are notoriously poor "tempo moves," i.e., the kind of moves that maintain the status quo. This is because each pawn move inherently alters the position forevermore. Never *voluntarily* move a pawn, *unless you are convinced that it stands better on the new square than on its original one*!

We shall start our discussion of pawn play with the most important concepts regarding the handling of the center. Let us set up the most common position in the closed treatment of the Ruy Lopez, after the moves 1 P–K4 P–K4 2 N–KB3 N–QB3 3 B–N5 P–QR3 4 B–R4 N–B3 5 0–0 B–K2 6 R–K1 P–QN4 7 B–N3 P–Q3 8 P–B3 0–0 9 P–KR3.

In the Closed Variation of the Ruy Lopez, Black's immediate strategic priority is to ensure that his central bastion, the KP, can hold its ground. White's last move has prepared a risk–free attack on Black's KP with 10 P–Q4. A popular continuation for Black now is the Breyer Variation ("Breyer's regrouping" would be a more accurate name).

DIAGRAM 45

BLACK

WHITE

Ruy Lopez
Closed Variation
after 9 P–KR3

9 . . . N–N1 10 P–Q4

The four primary central squares—already discussed in Chapter 1—are White's Q4 and K4 and Black's Q4 and K4. Let's for a few moments limit our central evaluations to the Queen and King files. We can arbitrarily (yet reasonably soundly) assign a value of two to a central pawn on the 4th rank and a value of one to a central pawn on the 3rd rank. Adding up the values here we get $2 + 2 = 4$ for White's central pawns and $1 + 2 = 3$ for Black's central pawns. White has more central pawn influence on an arithmetical basis (4 vs. 3) and also on a relative basis ($4 \div 3 = 1.33$).

10 . . . QN–Q2!

This is Breyer's idea. But let us consider what happens if Black plays 10 . . . PxP?. It may seem that Black is engaging in an equivalent exchange, i.e., giving up a KP on the 4th rank for White's QP on its fourth. Thus Black is left with $3 - 2 = 1$ unit of central pawns, and White is left with $4 - 2 = 2$ units. As before, the arithmetic difference is 1 unit. But there is a great change in the *relative* central influence. This now is $2 \div 1 = 2$, up considerably from the 1.33 *before* the exchange. Thus, on a *relative* basis White's central influence has been strengthened considerably.

The actual situation for Black will be even worse than the above calculation shows, because White, instead of recapturing with the Queen or KN, can play 11 PxP!. White then has $2 + 2 = 4$ units of central pawn power, whereas Black is left with only one unit. On an arithmetical basis White is ahead 3 units, and on a relative basis up by $4 \div 1 = 4$! We can now easily appreciate how disastrous for Black 10 . . . PxP? would be in central influence. Playing 10 . . . PxP is called "giving up the center." *Never, never give up the center unless you have no choice or you get something valuable in return.*

11 QN–Q2

White's normal move. What would be the result if, instead, White plays 11 PxP ?!? If Black recaptures by 11 . . . QNxP?! then everything is fine for White, with his arithmetic central pawn power being $4 - 2 = 2$, while Black's is $3 - 2 = 1$, and on a relative basis White has increased his influence to $2 \div 1 = 2$. However, note what happens if Black plays 11 . . . PxP!: now the position in the center is absolutely equivalent, with each side having 2 units there. Thus the exchange 11 PxP by White has led to both an absolute and relative decrease in White's central power. By playing 11 PxP (when Black can respond with 11 . . . PxP) White is said to "relieve central tension." On the face of it, this is a *disadvantageous operation. Never, never relieve the central tension unless you have no choice or gain something valuable in turn.*

After 11 QN–Q2 the normal variations ensue. Both sides will try to complete the development of the Queenside. For quite some time to come White will try to get Black to "give up the center," whereas Black will strive to force White to "relieve the central tension."

With the above background we can understand better the rationale for the main variation of the Slav Defense that we briefly considered in Chapter 7. After 1 P–Q4 P–Q4 2 P–QB4 P–QB3 3 N–QB3 N–B3 4 N–B3 Black "gave up the center" by playing 4 . . . PxP. However, he gained the following three items as compensation: (1) healthy development of his QB; (2) one developmental tempo, since White is "forced" to play the non-developmental 5 P–QR4; (3) permanent control of the QN5 square, which is potentially useful for the KB or QN.

The other important question is how to recapture when more than one pawn can do so. A characteristic situation is shown in Diagram 46, B. Spassky–A. Karpov, 1974 Match, Game #2, Caro–Kann Defense, after White's 12th move (1 P–K4 P–QB3 2 P–Q4 P–Q4 3 N–QB3 PxP 4 NxP B–B4 5 N–N3 B–N3 6 N–B3 N–Q2 7 B–Q3 P–K3 8 0–0 KN–B3 9 P–B4 B–Q3 10 P–N3 0–0 11 B–N2 P–B4 12 BxB).

DIAGRAM 46

BLACK

WHITE

Spassky–Karpov
1974 Match Game 2
after 12 B × B

12 . . . RPxB!

The general principle is very clear: *always* recapture *towards* the center, unless there is a *very good reason* to do otherwise. The logic is very sound: in our case the KRP is transformed into a KNP, and the control over the secondary central square KB4 is strengthened. Moreover, Black's pawn formation remains sound. In this situation 12 . . . BPxB?! would have two disadvantages: central influence is lessened and Black is left with an isolated and vulnerable KP. In the type of position shown in Diagram 46, there would be two

situations when recapture with the RP would be inferior: (1) if
White could launch a strong attack along the KR–file by doubling
major pieces there, (2) if Black could make extremely good use of
the opening of the KB–file. Since these conditions are not present
here, the only correct recapture is "toward the center."

The game was called a draw after the further moves 13 R–K1
Q–B2 14 PxP BxP 15 Q–B2 KR–Q1 16 N–K4 NxN 17 QxN—
though White remains with a slight advantage.

The kind of situation where it is more useful to recapture "away
from the center" is shown by the course of the game Y. Dorfman–Svedchikov, U.S.S.R. 1978, Benoni Defense:

1 P–Q4 N–KB3 2 P–QB4 P–B4 3 P–Q5 P–K3 4 N–QB3 PxP 5
PxP P–Q3 6 N–B3 P–KN3 7 P–K4 B–N2 8 B–KN5 P–KR3 9
B–R4 P–KN4?! 10 B–N3 N–R4 11 B–N5ch K–B1 12 P–K5! NxB
13 BPxN!

DIAGRAM 47

BLACK

WHITE

Dorfman–Svedchikov
USSR 1978
after 13 BP×N!

White, with his 11th and 12th moves, has launched a direct
attack against Black's King. Recapturing with the KBP is the only
logical follow-up, since White will now have the open KB–file to
attack Black's uncastled King. In the event of the "strategic" 13
RPxN?, Black would win a pawn for nothing with 13 . . . PxP.

13 . . . P–R3   14 B–Q3 PxP   15 0–0 P–N4   16 Q–K2 P–B5   17 NxKP!

Because of the strength of the plan associated with White's 12th and 13th moves, the sub-variation with 9 . . . P–KN4?! has disappeared from master praxis. White always gets a very strong attack—and usually wins. So also here.

17 . . . Q–N3ch   18 K–R1 PxB   19 Q–R5! K–N1   20 QxPch K–R2   21 P–Q6! QxP   22 N–K4! QxN   23 N–B6ch QxN   24 RxQ R–N1   25 RxKRPch KxR   26 QxR N–Q2   27 Q–Q5 R–R2   28 Q–B6ch N–B3   29 QxB R–K2   30 P–KR4! N–K5   31 K–R2 PxP   32 PxP B–K4ch   33 P–KN3! NxP   34 K–R3 B–Q3   35 Q–B8ch K–R2   36 QxRch BxQ   37 KxN B–B3   38 R–Q1 Black resigns

From a purely strategic standpoint the principle of pawns "capturing towards the center" is always sound. Yet very early in the opening other factors such as development are often of overriding importance. Consider the Exchange Variation of the Ruy Lopez: 1 P–K4 P–K4   2 N–KB3 N–QB3   3 B–N5 P–QR3   4 BxN. According to our principle, 4 . . . NPxB is the correct move. However, after that recapture Black has some trouble developing and guarding K4, factors which White can exploit with the active 5 P–Q4!. Therefore, best for Black is the "anticentral" 4 . . . QPxB!, since this furthers both the Queen's and QB's development, with 5 NxP?! being easily parried by 5 . . . Q–Q5!.

A similar consideration applies to the following line in the Nimzovitch Variation of the Sicilian Defense: 1 P–K4 P–QB4   2 N–KB3 N–KB3   3 P–K5 N–Q4   4 N–B3 NxN. From an immediate central outlook, 5 NPxN is correct, yet that gives Black the opportunity to annihilate White's K5 outpost with 5 . . . P–Q3 and obtain approximate equality. Considerably stronger for White is the developmental 5 QPxN!, since then 5 . . . P–Q3 can be met by 6 PxP!, and whether Black recaptures with 6 . . . PxP or 6 . . . QxP 7 QxQ PxQ, his QP will be a serious weakness.

The question of King safety must always be kept in mind when considering recaptures. For example, after 1 P–Q4 N–KB3   2 B–N5 P–Q4   3 BxN, how should Black recapture? If central influence were the only consideration, 3 . . . NPxB would be much the better way. Yet the KRP is then isolated, and the lack of the

KNP may make Black's King somewhat uncomfortable. Therefore, a majority of masters currently prefer the safe, sound, development 3 . . . KPxB.

The expression "pawn formation" simply means the position of the pawns as they stand on the board. Often the reference is to a particular section of the board, be it center, Kingside or Queenside. Always remember that an apparently slight change in a pawn formation can have a major fundamental effect. To illustrate this, let us look at a very common position in the King's Indian Defense: 1 P–Q4 N–KB3 2 P–QB4 P–KN3 3 N–QB3 B–N2 4 P–K4 P–Q3. In evaluating this position it is easy to see that White has a considerable central superiority, due to having three pawns on the fourth rank. Black, on the other hand, has concentrated on developing his Kingside and has just a bit of central pawn influence. White now has three perfectly logical continuations, each leading to a different central pawn formation:

1. Normal Variation: 5 N–B3 0–0 6 B–K2. Here White says that he is completely satisfied with what he already has in the center.

2. Sämisch Variation: 5 P–B3 0–0 6 B–K3. White wants to secure his center and therefore plays 5 P–B3. The "Sämisch" is not a sharp attacking variation, but a strategic way of trying to ensure that White will remain with a central and spatial advantage.

3. Four Pawns Attack: 5 P–B4 0–0 6 N–B3. White is not satisfied with "only" having three pawns on the fourth rank in the center and wants to have four pawns there! This is a very sharp try at overwhelming Black with early central pawn advances. Yet note that White has neglected his piece development and his center with four pawns abreast has no safe base of support.

In none of the variations we considered above did White have anything which can be called a structural pawn–formation weakness. Clearly his KP is unvulnerable to attack, and therefore Black must look for his central counterplay by challenging White's QP. In the Normal and Sämisch Variations, both . . . P–QB4 and . . . P–K4 look logical, but actual experience has shown that the . . . P–K4 advance is the more effective one. In the Four Pawns Attack, White's KBP has essentially prevented Black's . . . P–K4, but here . . . P–QB4 (e.g., 6 . . . P–B4!) gives excellent counterplay.

However, there are variations—even popular ones—where one side starts off with a fundamental structural weakness. One of the main lines in the Najdorf Variation of the Sicilian Defense goes as follows: 1 P–K4 P–QB4 2 N–KB3 P–Q3 3 P–Q4 PxP 4 NxP N–KB3 5 N–QB3 P–QR3 6 B–K2 P–K4 7 N–N3—see Diagram 48.

DIAGRAM 48

BLACK

WHITE

Sicilian Defense
Najdorf Variation
after 7 N–N3

As a result of 6 . . . P–K4, Black has both chased White's KN away from the center and gained definite central presence himself.

Yet there also are two negative features to Black's central advance. Firstly, the QP has become a "backward" pawn—i.e., one which is vulnerable to a frontal attack and incapable of a ready advance. As can be seen, the KB will have to remain on the inactive K2 square just to keep the QP sufficiently protected. The second negative is that Black's Q4 has been permanently weakened, since Black has no pawn remaining which can protect that square.

Because of these negative features, there are many strong players who do not play 6 . . . P–K4 after White's 6 B–K2. They prefer either 6 . . . P–K3, transposing into the Scheveningen Variation, where Black has good control of his Q4 square or—despite the tempo lost with 5 . . . P–QR3—6 . . . P–KN3, transposing into the Dragon Variation. In each instance, the structural weaknesses in Black's pawn formation are considerably less than after 6 . . . P–K4.

Good pawn play requires that we don't voluntarily create weak pawns. Weak pawns are those that are isolated, doubled or backward. As a matter of principle, these should be avoided— unless something valuable is gained in return.

An "isolated" pawn is one by itself, i.e., with no pawn on either of the adjoining files. A characteristic situation results from the following line of the Tarrasch Variation of the French Defense: 1 P–K4 P–K3 2 P–Q4 P–Q4 3 N–Q2 P–QB4 4 KPxP KPxP 5 B–N5ch N–QB3 6 KN–B3 B–Q3 7 PxP BxBP 8 0–0 KN–K2 9 N–N3 B–Q3—see Diagram 49.

DIAGRAM 49

BLACK

WHITE

French Defense
Tarrasch Variation
after 9 . . . B–Q3

It is easy to see that Black's QP is fundamentally weak, since there is no other pawn that can support it. In this case Black hopes that the central squares covered by the QP, coupled with the generally free and harmonious development of the minor pieces will be sufficient compensation for the pawn's inherent weakness.

"Doubled pawns" need not be inherently weak, apart from the obvious weakness of *isolated* doubled pawns. Doubled pawns as part of a pawn cluster may be perfectly satisfactory for defensive purposes. Their major problem is lack of potency in the offense. In the first place, as they advance, they can easily leave large gaps in their former territory. Secondly, there is the problem of not being able to create a passed pawn from certain pawn–majority formations containing doubled pawns. A formerly much–played line in the Exchange Variation of the Ruy Lopez opens as follows: 1 P–K4 P–K4 2 N–KB3 N–QB3 3 B–N5 P–QR3 4 BxN QPxB 5 P–Q4 PxP 6 QxP QxQ 7 NxQ. Though the game has just begun, the characteristic pawn formations are already established: on the Kingside White has a four–pawn vs. three–pawn majority, and it is a "mobile" majority, meaning that White—if he wishes—can create a passed pawn there. On the Queenside Black has a four–pawn vs. three–pawn majority, yet Black's majority is a static one. It's fine for defensive purposes, but not of much usefulness for offense. If White plays his Queenside pawns correctly, there is no way that Black can force a passed pawn there. For instance, if the QR– and QN– pawns are exchanged, what we are left with are two QBPs for Black and one QBP for White—and offensively Black has gotten nowhere. There is no question that in the position after 7 NxQ White has the superior pawn formation. As compensation for this Black must seek open lines and good development for his pieces, in particular his pair of Bishops.

The "backward" pawn was already briefly addressed earlier in this chapter when discussing the line in the Najdorf Variation of the Sicilian Defense resulting after 6 B–K2 P–K4. There, Black voluntarily accepted the backward pawn in exchange for increased influence over his K4 and Q5 squares. As a general principle, however, backward pawns should be avoided because not only are they potentially vulnerable to a frontal attack, but they are also immobile. Let us look at the following schematic diagram of Queenside pawns: White has a two–pawn vs. one–pawn Queenside pawn majority, but how to mobilize it? Wrong is 1 P–QR4?, because this immediately fixes White's QNP as backward, since it cannot advance to N4 in safety. Equally wrong is 1 P–QR3? since after 1 . . . P–R5! White QNP is again backward and incapable of advance. Note how in each of these two cases,

Black's single pawn is able to contain two White pawns. The correct way to mobilize the Queenside pawns is 1 P–QN3 followed by 2 P–QR3! and 3 P–N4. Then White is assured of what he wants: creating a passed pawn from his normal pawn majority.

DIAGRAM 50

BLACK

WHITE

Schematic diagram of
Queenside Pawns

The pawn weaknesses discussed so far—isolated, doubled, backward pawns—are the most important *structural* weaknesses. What is also important to understand is the concept of *dynamic* pawn weaknesses. As a pawn advances from its starting position it becomes more accessible to attack by enemy pawns and pieces. Of course, most of the time this is nothing to worry about. However, pawn advances in the vicinity of one's own King must always be handled with extreme care. If a direct attack against the King can be anticipated, then it is better to not touch the pawns in front of the King at all. Typical examples of the right and wrong way are shown arising from the following line of the Scheveningen Variation of the Sicilian Defense: 1 P–K4 P–QB4 2 N–KB3 P–K3 3 P–Q4 PxP 4 NxP N–KB3 5 N–QB3 P–Q3 6 B–QB4 B–K2 7 B–N3 0–0 8 B–K3 N–R3 9 P–B3 N–B4 10 Q–Q2 P–QR3 11 P–N4—see Diagram 51.

DIAGRAM 51

BLACK

WHITE

Scheveningen Variation
Sicilian Defense
after 11 P–N4

Without question, White has started a direct attack against Black's castled King position. Further, it can be anticipated that White himself will *not* castle on the Kingside. (Most probably White will castle on the Queenside.) White's immediate plan is to dislodge Black's well–placed KN with 12 P–N5. What—if anything—should Black do about this threat? Two approaches are plausible.

- A) *Wrong is:* 11 . . . P–R3?, since after 12 P–KR4! followed by 13 P–N5, not only will Black's Knight be chased away, anyway, but, even more important, the advance of Black's KRP means that White will be able to force open a line against Black's King.
- B) *The right way* is to leave the Kingside alone and to get ready for counterplay on the Queenside. Logical, therefore, is 11 . . . Q–B2! 12 P–N5 N/3–Q2 13 P–KR4 P–N4!. The position remains very double-edged, of course, yet extensive master practice has shown that Black's chances are in no way inferior to White's.